THE TRUTH ABOUT LUCK

Also by the Author

One Bird's Choice

THE TRUTH ABOUT LUCK

WHAT I LEARNED ON MY ROAD TRIP WITH GRANDMA

IAIN REID

ANANSI

This edition published in 2013 by
House of Anansi Press Inc.
110 Spadina Avenue, Suite 801
Toronto, ON, M5V 2K4
Tel. 416-363-4343
Fax 416-363-1017
www.houseofanansi.com

Distributed in Canada by
HarperCollins Canada Ltd.
1995 Markham Road
Scarborough, ON, M1B 5M8
Toll free tel. 1-800-387-0117

Distributed in the United States by
Publishers Group West
1700 Fourth Street
Berkeley, CA 94710
Toll free tel. 1-800-788-3123

House of Anansi Press is committed to protecting our natural environment. As part of our efforts, the interior of this book is printed on paper that contains 100% post-consumer recycled fibres, is acid-free, and is processed chlorine-free.

17 16 15 14 13   1 2 3 4 5

Library and Archives Canada Cataloguing in Publication

Reid, Iain, 1981–
The truth about luck : what I learned on my road trip with
grandma / Iain Reid.

Also issued in electronic format.
ISBN 978-1-77089-241-5

1. Reid, Iain, 1981-. 2. Grandparent and child. 3. Authors, Canadian (English)—21st century—Biography. 4. Canadian wit and humour (English). I. Title.

HQ759.9.R43 2013   306.874'5092   C2012-905955-2

Library of Congress Control Number: 2012948142

Cover design: Alysia Shewchuk
Text design and typesetting: Alysia Shewchuk

Canada Council   Conseil des Arts
for the Arts   du Canada

ONTARIO ARTS COUNCIL
CONSEIL DES ARTS DE L'ONTARIO

We acknowledge for their financial support of our publishing program the Canada Council for the Arts, the Ontario Arts Council, and the Government of Canada through the Canada Book Fund.

Printed and bound in Canada

RECYCLED
Paper made from
recycled material
FSC® C103567

To Grandma

"Time just gets away from us."
— Charles Portis, *True Grit*

IN MAY 1943, the Canadian nursing sisters of the six-hundred-bed No. 5 General, stationed in Taplow, England, were abruptly informed their unit would be moving out. They didn't know where, only that it was imminent. The plan was to act on the recent success of the Tunisia Campaign. The Allied forces had gained control over the coast of North Africa. Within a few weeks all remaining patients in the hospital had been transferred. The wards were closed.

For the preceding four weeks the nurses drilled, marched, attended lectures, and practised raising tents. Along with being issued gas masks, they were taught how to prevent malaria. It seemed likely they were headed some-where warm. Less than two weeks after the Allied invasion of Sicily had begun — the front lines only a few, short miles to the north — amidst heavy shelling, the nurses of No. 5 General landed at Augusta.

Between 1943 and 1945, over ninety-two thousand Canadians fought in the Italian Campaign. The environ-ment was harsh. It was unmanageably hot. The ground was mountainous. Disease thrived. Supplies were scarce. Rations were few. Nearly six thousand Canadians were killed. It was Canada's largest loss in any one country during the Second World War.

It also marked the first time Canadian nurses served in an active theatre of war.

THIRTY-EIGHT YEARS LATER, in the spring of 1981, a gaunt baby boy was born three weeks premature in a secure Ottawa hospital. The placenta had pulled away from the wall of the uterus. His mother was rushed to hospital, where an emergency C-section was performed. Mother lost a lot of blood and required a transfusion. Baby was fine. Both were lucky to survive.

He was a strikingly gangly infant, only five pounds, three ounces, but long and lanky. He had an asymmetrical dimple on his chin and was crowned by a large, domed skull carpeted with fine blond hair. All agreed he had extraordinarily skinny legs and the substantially adult ears of Walter Matthau.

Most of his five pounds and three ounces was probably found in those fleshy ears.

MONDAY

8:12 a.m.

IT DOESN'T ALWAYS drip. It usually does, but not always. This morning: it's dripping. A new drop emerges every three seconds. I'm drooped on the toilet, monitoring the tap like a lifeguard. Not to worry, the seat is down. I'm clothed, reasonably. I'm wearing underwear — plaid boxer shorts with a tiny horizontal rip below my left hip. I'm using the toilet as a chair (not as a toilet), a porcelain La-Z-Boy minus the padded features. The floor is cold on my feet. I'm missing my slippers.

I've decided I actually don't mind this drip. Mostly I hate drips of any sort. This one's gentle. It's calming. As far as drips go, it's almost nerdy. You can't even hear it outside the bathroom. Not if you're more than two and a half steps away. With the door closed. While whistling "Uptown Girl."

I came in to brush my teeth and splash a handful or two of water onto my face. I didn't even make it to the tube of paste before calling an audible and just sitting. The rear of the toilet, the rectangular tank part, is cold like the floor and makes for a terrible backrest. I catch a glimpse of myself in the mirror. My gruesome slouch has formed my spine into the letter *C*. It's almost as if the engineers forgot about this usage, toilet as chair, when they designed it. I'm hunched over, uneasily, my right foot resting on my left knee. I'm using my arm as a pillar to hold up my head. I'm in a traditional "thinker" pose, in a contemporary setting.

But there's more to do today than think. It's just after 8 a.m., still early. I have planning to do and tasks to carry out. Tasks — there's something I dislike more than drips. Tasks and errands. I'm not much of a doer, or man of action. I'll just sit here a bit longer. A dull ache somewhere in my prefrontal cortex isn't helping. It's really more of a rear-eye ache. Why do my eyes hurt? Could that be a muscular thing? I hope it's not vascular.

Okay, fine, there is one thing I resent about this drip: its Terminator-like discipline. No drip ever misses its turn, or even shows up late. Never. Unlike me, it's contrary to cunctation. Every three seconds. There it goes again. And again. Drip . . . drip.

The planning I *should* be doing is for a trip of sorts, a trip that's meant to start soonish, i.e., later today. I realize the planning should have been done by now, before the first day of the trip. I've had more than three months to ensure it will be a trip light on banalities and full of adventure. The problem is, I kept putting it off because I knew today was three months away.

When it's laid out in front of you, three months is a rambling cornfield of time, rows and rows of tall, green stalks between you and the ninetieth day. For me, *three months* is a synonym for *eternity*. It's so long, I'm still resisting the planning. I'm putting it off as you read this. Three months ago the trip seemed like three years away, three lifetimes.

And then suddenly you wake up with a disconcerting eye ache and today is here and today has become today. I should make a list of what still needs to be done. Lists equate to efficiency, productivity.

Why does it drip so consistently? Its self-mastery makes me think of a particularly adroit marine. I guess it makes sense, though; it would be illogical if it was erratic. Drips aren't like people. If I made more lists could I be a marine? I do have short hair.

Even though it always sticks up at the back at two particular spots, like horns, I don't mind my early-morning hair. I can live with its undeviating sloppiness. But I've never warmed to my morning eyes. It's the entire circumference of both eyes that is unusually puffy, not just the bottom pouches. My morning eyes are what eyes would look like if eyes could yawn. They stay in this unbecoming form, holding the yawn, inflamed and wilted all at once, for much longer than they need to. Definitely longer than most people's morning eyes, which are often cute and fleeting. Coupled with my morning horns, I unfairly appear to have just risen from sleep an hour or two after lunch. My eyes can't look like this because I'm tired. I just slept for nine hours. Maybe it means I'm dehydrated? Or could it be vascular?

About this trip: it's changed. So it's really not just that I've been putting off the planning, but that it continues to (d)evolve. There's a metaphor here about a caterpillar and a cocoon, a brightly coloured butterfly and a poorly organized, disappointing trip. At first, it was going to be somewhere far, exotic. There would be a plane, or planes, and trains involved. Maybe a rickety bus with satchels roped onto the roof. There would be spicy meals served with thick mango juice and fresh seafood, and certainly hotels — fancy ones. And paper maps spread out over the table in our room. Maybe a heated pool and a beach or two. We would need proper hiking boots but also waterproof sandals. A camera would be required to take exciting-looking photos of us participating in inspiring activities that we could later print and frame on our walls or fridge.

Early on I made the mistake of telling her she'd probably need her bathing suit. "You'll probably need your bathing suit," I said. Not anymore. I guess it's still going to be a trip, but barely. It's like a hammock — fun to nap on for an hour or two, but it's hardly a bed.

In that sense the trip is like a toilet seat, too.

I should probably wash the mirror above the tap. From this angle I'm noticing some scuff marks, smudges, and fingerprints. That won't be nice for her to see. It's strange, I have no memory of ever touching the bathroom mirror, yet I'm staring at a streaked fingerprint. Maybe it's just too bright in here. It's so bright my hair looks thinner than it really is. I can see my scalp. From an evolutionary perspective, I feel like thin hair in any light should be considered attractive, no? Doesn't it mean an abundant supply of testosterone? And doesn't that mean Good Things?

As of this morning the trip's going to be little more than a road trip, a paltry road trip. It's going to be the fucking Cold War of vacations, lots of build-up and flashy rhetoric with no action. I'm the Gorbachev of trip planning. The worst part is, it's not even for me. A minor road trip would easily fulfill *my* trip quota for years. It's for someone else. It was a gift. The gift was advertised and offered as a proper holiday.

I need to get going. Or at least get off this toilet. Or at least start a list. I'm starting to compose one now. Mentally. One battle at a time.

First I need to stand. Which I do, stretching my back as I step over to the sink. My ankles are stiff. I've been noticing this every morning for the past month or so. It makes sense because I'm getting older. I'm at an age where most people are getting cozy with adult life. This is a common age to be married, to start a family. I'm not doing any of these things, but I am aging. Getting older means I'm probably going to have an accident, tear my Achilles tendon while walking to the store or something. Achilles tears are one of the most common injuries in men my age, men whose tendons are slowly turning from elastic to rope.

I cough once and twist the left tap marked with the stylized *h*. I'm waiting for the water to get to *h*. I've waited for hot water to fall from the tap the past two mornings. Even though the hot water tank has been broken for the past two mornings. Right, it's still broken today. That's all I can tell you about it. I have no diagnosis. I need to call someone about that.

I also have to clean the car. That's definitely a priority. And check the oil, fill up the windshield washer reservoir, and stabilize the air pressure in all four tires. I'll need to mobilize our supplies.

I walk over to the shower just to kick the grungy plastic curtain. I'm not going to shower. I have too many things to do. I'm just too busy for this type of extended grooming. Also, I don't have hot water.

I walk back to the sink. The cold water's still spilling out of the tap wastefully. I bend down, splashing some onto my face. Maybe the cold water will help wake my eyes. I twist it shut and let the water trickle down off my nose. This time the drip doesn't return. I don't understand. I wait, but it's gone. Maybe for good this time.

There are some whiskers dried onto the sides of the porcelain bowl from my shave last night. It makes the sink look like the floor of a minuscule barber shop. I rise up slowly and examine my eyes in the mirror. No noticeable improvement. From this close, it's ridiculous how long my lashes are. They're farcically long and feminine.

I have to get going. But seriously, the light is definitely too bright. I prefer a humble bulb, one with nothing to prove and a little less wattage. I swallow some saliva. I hope it's not cloudy outside.

I need to get more sun.

9:41 a.m.

I LIVE IN a small city and rarely use my car. Not just because it's old and ugly and unreliable and deafening but because I can walk most places I need to go. I got it while living in a different city, a larger city, where I worked at an office and drove every day. I haven't driven it in a couple of weeks and am pleasantly surprised. It's in better shape than anticipated. There's less crap scattered throughout than I remembered. Only enough to half-fill one small plastic bag. Killing two birds with one stone, I do this while nibbling a toasted bagel smeared in herb-and-garlic cream cheese. There's a muddy Frisbee on the middle back seat, along with a box of empty CD cases and lots of paper receipts.

I hide all this in the trunk, where I find a musty duck-feather duvet and a porcelain coffee mug with the name Ken written on the side. I've been looking for this mug for over a year. Man, I love my Ken mug. It's such a great fucking mug! For now I leave it in the trunk.

Structurally the exterior is in good shape. There are only two patches of rust above the rear tire wells. And a couple of spherical dents on the hood that, for me, are attractive in the same way as a set of dimples. Two of the four hubcaps have been stolen, or fell off while I was driving. There are some superficial scratches on the side panel, but what twenty-year-old car nearing three hundred thousand kilometres doesn't have some scratches and a touch of rust? Along with the faded blue paint it's also wearing a thin coat of dirt. Cars are always dirty on the outside this time of year. There's just so much mud on the roads. I've also never washed it.

It's almost warm enough this morning to do just that. Do people still wash cars? I feel like that was more of a eighties thing. I could soap up a bucket of tepid water and slip into something apropos, swimming trunks or a snug pair of cut-off jeans. I'd get some of those monster sponges and just go to town with one in each hand. Then again, I don't think she'll care if it's a little muddy.

A neighbour walks by with her toddlers in tow. The children don't notice me standing in my shorts, hoodie, and slippers. The mother smiles and waves politely. This is the extent of our relationship. Waves and deferential smiles. Still I panic and return her greeting coarsely, by holding up my unassuming bag of paper trash like a talisman. She bends her head and says something indecipherable to the kids. They continue on. Alone again, I crawl back inside the car.

I feel like I'm entering a hot blue metal cave with an automatic transmission. My first move is to pucker my lips and aim a spurt of breath at the field of dust living on the dash. With a few more spurts I'm lightheaded. Most of the dust has endured my gusty assault.

Resourcefully I fish my breakfast paper towel from my pocket and use it to wipe off the rest. That's when I see some cracker crumbs (or potentially breakfast-bagel crumbs) squatting in the crease on the passenger seat. I swipe them passively onto the floor. The passenger seat has to be clean. But so does the back seat. I'm still not sure where she's going to feel most comfortable.

Admittedly, even "clean," it lacks some pomp. But our chariot is ready. As I worm my way out backwards, one of my slippers, the left one, falls off onto the driveway. I remain kneeling across the front seats and go fishing for it blindly with the now bare foot. I'm able to catch a few small bits of gravel that stick to my sole, but no slipper.

I wonder if she'll want to do any of the driving?

12:18 p.m.

I HAVEN'T VISITED Lilac Hill, my parents' hobby farm, in months. It's the same farm where I grew up and also returned to live for a year as an adult in my mid-twenties. I'm always pleased to see the old house again, the barns, fields, trees, and animals, too. Sometimes I will drive up for a day or two, just for the quiet, for the chance to walk through the fields without human interaction. Today everything looks too green and healthy for this early in the spring. There are embryonic buds on the lilac bushes and apple trees.

From the gate, there's no sign of the sheep or the chickens. The first sign of life that isn't perennial is the lone guinea fowl, Lucius. I got to know Lucius and his abrasive personality well the year I returned to the farm. His long neck is stretched upward, his wings tucked into his sides as he sprints up to the verandah from the back field. Lucius sprints? This is new. His legs are shamefully thin and remind me of pink matchsticks. Why doesn't he just fly? Wouldn't it be easier *and* faster?

He joins Titan, the guard dog, who yawns and lumbers over to greet me. Titan pushes his entire face past the door as I knee it open. It feels like a furry brick on my lap. Like me, he's looking older. There's more grey in his snout. He probably thought his bathroom light (the morning sun) was too bright this morning, too.

Lucius tiptoes around to the front of the car. I hear him snacking, pecking at the dead bugs freckled across the licence plate and bumper. I say hi to Titan and rub behind his ears and his neck. I stand. "Lucius," I say, and nod sourly at the ugly bird. Although housemates for a full year, we never really hit it off. He chirps his reply and tilts his curved beak to the right, peering up at me.

Inside I find Mom at the kitchen table. Even when she's seated, it's easy to discern her diminutive stature. She's around five feet tall and likely shrinking with age. Her short, undyed greying hair is still askew from sleep. She's wearing one of Dad's massive fleece vests over her clothes. She's staring blankly ahead and grinning widely. "Oh, Iain, what a surprise. What are you doing here? Aren't you going on your big trip today?"

"Yeah, yeah. I just came by to pick up a few things. And it's not going to be big anymore."

"I'll put some more coffee on," she says, standing to stack and carry the breakfast dishes over to the sink. "I just finished the last cup. Are you cold in here? I find it cold today, that's why I'm wearing so many layers."

"I'm fine, but what's so funny?"

"What? I wasn't smiling."

"Yes, you were."

"Really?"

"Definitely."

"Oh, well, I guess I was just thinking of something that happened in the night — with your dad."

Here I feel obliged to stick my head into the freezer. "Okay, okay," I say, grimacing, raising both hands defensively.

"No, no. This was actually quite funny."

"Oh?"

"At some point in the night I got up to use the bathroom.

And when I came back, I saw all the covers were balled up on Dad's side and he was all twisted up in them. He looked like a big cabbage roll or something." She starts laughing now and takes a full minute, or two, to compose herself. "Anyway, I just hate crawling back into a mess like that, so I very gently started to straighten them. Well, you'd think he'd been tipped out of a dump truck. He swung his leg over and then half fell out of the bed and grabbed the side of the dresser. I mean, come on, how could I possibly have the strength to move your dad like that?"

Dad is a tall man, well over six feet.

"So you think he was subconsciously embellishing?"

"Well, I'm just saying. It doesn't add up."

"Interesting."

"He does have a flair for the dramatic when woken up in the middle of the night."

"True."

"I couldn't fall back asleep 'cause I was chuckling about it, I mean real belly laughs. I was trying not to. I don't think Dad fell back asleep for a while, either, just on account of the shock and my laughing."

"An eventful night, indeed. Where is the big guy?"

"Who, Titan? He's outside, didn't you see him when —" Mom stands now, walking toward the door, concerned for her dog's whereabouts.

"No, Mom, not Titan. *Dad*. Where's your tall husband?"

"Sorry, yes, Dad. He's at the feed mill getting grain."

Mom's cat Pumpkin is now circling her feet. I hadn't noticed him enter. "What do you want, Pecan? You heard me stand up, didn't you."

"Pecan?"

"His new nickname," answers Mom. "You knew that, didn't you?"

"No, but I must say, Pecan is looking decent for an old cat. Much better than at Christmas."

My compliment aimed at her senior cat lifts up Mom's face and head like they're attached to hundreds of miniature balloons. "Oh," she beams, "I know, I think so, too. It's amazing. He's doing so well." She bends down slowly and scratches along his spine. "I have a secret weapon that's turned his health around."

"I know, Mom. I've given him his insulin shots before, I know all about it."

"Well, yeah, there's that, but I'm talking about something else." She shuffles over to the fridge. She moves a few things around, humming to herself. "Here," she says, "found it."

She walks back to me and holds up a plastic container an inch from my face. I have to lean back to make the label legible. "Yogurt!?"

"YO-gurt," she says. "Plain yogurt. He ab-so-lute-ly loves it. And I'm convinced it's making all the difference. His coat is better, his eyes are better, his posture —"

"Let me guess, better?"

"Do you want to see him scarf some up?"

"Tempting —"

The door creaks open, and in walks Dad. I'm tall, but Dad's taller and larger. I switch from looking down at Mom to up at Dad. He's wearing an old ball cap, jeans, and a blue plaid jacket. "Hey, bud. What are you doing here?"

"Just stopping by quickly to say hi — oh, and I might borrow a few things — and get caught up on Pecan, of course."

"Have you heard about the yogurt?" He says this earnestly, but simultaneously glances over at Mom and spots the yogurt container in her hand. He nods at the answer to his own question. "Well, I hope you don't have to sleep here. Trust me, Mom won't let you get a full night's sleep."

"Oh, come on, stop it," says Mom, putting the yogurt down on the table with authority. "I was just telling Iain all about it."

Dad removes his cap, scratches his head. He takes a step closer. "You should have seen what she did to me last night." It's obvious Mom's restraining her grin by biting her bottom lip. "She grabbed me by the ankle and thrust me out of bed in the middle of the night as if there were a fire. My foot hit the floor. I could barely stay in the bed."

"Come on! I didn't even touch you. I barely moved the blanket and off you went."

I've started to discreetly exit the kitchen, backing away gently.

"Where are you going?" asks Mom. They stare at me as if I'm the sole arbiter and a verdict is needed.

"Sorry, guys, I just came by to get a few things."

"Can't you stay for lunch or a walk?" Dad's standing over the fruit bowl.

"No, I better not. I'm already a bit late. And I shouldn't keep her waiting."

"Oh, right," says Mom. "And I'm sure she'll be happy to treat you for lunch somewhere."

"Well, probably, but the point is, it's a trip for her, so

really I should be doing most if not all of the treating." As I'm speaking, I wander over to the liquor cabinet and tip a liberal portion of Dad's favourite Croft Sherry into my metal water bottle. "I can't be frugal." I've already sloshed in about a third of the bottle when he notices.

"What are you doing with my sherry?" he asks.

"Oh." I stop. "Well, it's really not for me, Dad, it's for her." I tip another shot into my bottle, keeping my eyes on him. "She enjoys the odd glass. It'll be a nice treat on the trip."

"She does enjoy a little sherry as a treat every now and then," confirms Mom, bending down to pick up Pumpkin. "And it's her trip."

Dad just raises his eyebrows, turning back to his fruit. "I suppose."

12:49 p.m.

I'VE COME BY the farm to gather provisions for our trip. I should have planned this better. I should have started earlier. I didn't.

Considering these shortfalls, I'm satisfied with my hoard. Along with the dry sherry, I've neatly filled a dented blue Coleman cooler with a half-eaten box of Triscuits, a knob of old cheddar, three carrots, a few bags of pekoe tea, a stick of unsalted butter, and a pound of frozen ground lamb. I put some ice cubes in a Ziploc bag and toss them on top. Things are looking up.

"You need anything else?" asks Mom. "We've got loads of coffee. What about honey? Or eggs?"

"Wait, I thought you guys were going on a trip," says Dad. "Why are you pillaging us?"

"Yeah, we are — sort of."

"Whatever that means," says Dad, retreating to his study, coffee in one hand, an apple in the other.

"What does that mean?" asks Mom a few minutes later, when I'm ready to leave. "*Sort of* a trip?"

"Nothing," I say. "Thanks for the stuff. I better get going."

"Well, have fun!"

"Right." I pick up my cooler, feeling all my precisely arranged food tumble into disarray. "I'm off."

"Enjoy! Enjoy! Bon voyage!" says Mom, walking me outside. "You've got a nice day for it."

When I finish packing the car, I see Dad stroll out from the house, too. "I'll grab the gate for you," he says, putting on his cap.

"Thanks."

"By the way, have you fixed your windshield wipers yet?"

"Not wipers, Dad, wiper. It's only one that's broken."

"But it's the driver's side, isn't it?"

"Yes."

"I thought you said last month you were going to get a new one."

"I thought I was. I intended to."

"What about your licence plate? You're still just taping it? I nod.

"Well, enjoy your trip," he says, heading down to the gate. "Show her a good time."

I get inside and start up the car. I know, I know, I should have put on a new wiper and properly fixed the plate. I also should have mended the exhaust. It sounds more like a backhoe than a car.

I start slowly down the lane, peering at the rear-view mirror. I'm fearful Lucius will reappear and dance in front of the car the way he is wont to do. The maniacal bird will strut back and forth, back and forth, for as long he feels is appropriate. It's indescribably frustrating. Thankfully I don't see him. Titan is sound asleep on his blanket by the verandah. He must be dreaming. It looks like his heavy legs are twitching. The sun is hidden behind one massive cloud that stretches lengthwise across the sky.

From so far away, this cloud looks to be around the size of Ireland. Along with its girth, it has that unmistakable feeling of impending rain.

IT WAS ABOUT four months ago when the idea for this trip was initially floated. It was late October or early November, near her birthday, maybe a week before. I was sitting at the Manx Pub in downtown Ottawa, nursing an ale with my older brother, Jimmy. It was a dreary fall night. I'd worn the Icelandic wool sweater my sister (who lives in Iceland) had given me for Christmas.

The Manx was packed. The scratched wooden tables were full of glasses, white plates, and silver cutlery, and groups huddled at the door, waiting their turn to eat and imbibe. We hadn't been seated long. I was already regretting my foolishly thermal attire. The bulky sweater was meant for the windy and wet Icelandic pastures, not a cozy pub well above capacity. Sitting across from me in his cotton

T-shirt, Jimmy commented twice on how he'd hit the perfect internal temperature. I dragged the back of my hand along my forehead.

For the past handful of years, when dealing with family gifts, Jimmy and I would receive separately, but we gave as a single entity. We were a gift-giving tandem, a beautiful hybridity of ingenuity and prudence. Perhaps what we produced was predictable and underwhelming, but we had each other.

Often we made things. Twice we sat for self-portraits. Dressing up for the portraits made them decidedly giftier. I would choose and create our costumes. Jimmy would construct frames from pieces of scrap wood found at our parents' farm. We would position ourselves about five feet from the digital camera we'd set up on a bookshelf. Two years ago we dressed as the main characters from *Brideshead Revisited*. I grew Charles Ryder's beard. Jimmy carried Sebastian's teddy bear, Aloysius.

This year Jimmy severed our network. He selfishly decided it was time to expand his gift basket into his own private, improved basket. It was at the Manx that he broke the news. I (metaphorically) cupped the back of his neck, pulling him toward me, and (literally) urged him to reconsider. But he'd already bought his gifts. I felt ridiculous. What was I going to do with two (very) authentic *Nicholas Nickleby* outfits?

Swirling the foamy beer around in his glass, Jimmy continued his onslaught, describing his already procured gifts. It was like listening to a graphic summation of your ex's new, better-looking, richer, non-perspiring lover, minutes after she's dumped you. Ultimately, I had to agree; most of the gifts were complete and thorough improvements over our shitty portraits. And besides, a solo portrait wouldn't be the end of the world.

Jimmy wondered who would build the frame. Fine, it didn't have to be a portrait. There were lots of things I could get her for her birthday.

"What about a scented candle?" I asked. "I feel like she loves candles. AND different scents."

"I guess that would be all right," shrugged Jimmy. "You look irritated. Are you hot? Why don't you take that sweater off? You look like a Maritime cod fisherman."

"I'm fine." I was teetering toward combustion.

Jimmy had starting texting. Or someone was texting him. The point is, he was focused on his phone. So I tried to picture her face when she unwrapped a heavily scented, waxy, pumpkin-spiced candle.

A minute later I slapped the table with both hands. "Or what about if I just made something, like some sort of — biscuit — or a loaf! Seriously, man, I feel like she's totally into loaves, right?"

Jimmy used one eye to look up from his phone for an eighth of a second. "Loavesofwhat?"

"I don't know, like a lemon loaf or a banana bread."

Then he looked directly at me. "Do you own a loaf pan?"

"I could *buy* one."

"But are you actually going to?"

"You know what," I said, tapping my temple with my index finger, "I saw this crazy tablecloth at the mall last week. It was brilliant, totally eye-catching. It was just remarkably zany, all covered in grapes and fruit and fucking pine cones. All kinds of different, unique, and very, very interesting shit. A real smorgasbord. I think there were vines and maybe some ivy. And it was plastic, right, which would be *soooooo* easy for her to keep clean."

Jimmy looked at me like I'd asked him to pull my finger.

I pushed my glass away. This worrying about gifts was a new, uninvited feeling. I'd been feeling it for about ten minutes but was already unimpressed and resentful. I'd never understood the requisite stress others felt about giving gifts. I'd always just waited until a day or two before, and inevitably the magic would happen.

And if it wasn't for Grandma's birthday, I wouldn't have been concerned this year, either. My maternal grandma, now in her nineties, was at an age when each birthday could (realistically) be her last.

Mine is a small family. None of my aunts and uncles are married, or have children. Myself, Jimmy, and our sister, Jean, have no cousins. Grandma is our last grandparent left. She's our only elderly relative. Her own family was large, with many siblings, aunts, and uncles. She was born in the northern tip of Scotland in the room above the corner store where her mother worked. Her family moved to Canada when she was two years old. They settled in Winnipeg. Her dad, a baker in Scotland, found work as a school custodian in Canada.

Her parents, her siblings have all died, most of them before what we would now consider old age. I think one of her sisters died in childbirth. George, her husband of almost fifty years, died in his eighties. That was more than fifteen years ago. Grandma is the last of her generation.

Growing up, we saw a lot of Grandma. It was impossible for her to visit the farm without edible treats, usually in the form of doughnuts. If the school bus dropped me off and I saw her car, my usual slow stroll up the lane became an energy-expending gallop. She knew each of our favourites, and there was always a vanilla-sprinkle waiting for me in the dozen.

She would regularly host family dinner parties where Grandpa would make Campari-infused cocktails for the adults and Grandma would construct unrestrained spreads involving "nibblies," appetizers, roasted meat, veggies, potatoes, salads, wines, and always a dessert. Even at lunch, Grandma always had a homemade sweet. Grandpa had a sweet tooth. So did Grandma. Her cookies were thin and crispy masterworks. Of all her scratch-made pies and tarts, I liked her lemon meringue, with its tall and curly peaks, the best.

It was Grandma who would organize games before supper, most of which she had invented. One of her best concoctions was the aptly named "Funny Walks," where each participant had to stroll across the room in such an unorthodox/unique/funny way as to make the others laugh. The more creative and absurd, the better. Grandma was the creator and Funny Walks master.

Grandma was always delicately cheerful. She seemed to be laughing a lot but almost more to herself, never garishly, like she knew a deeper (and funnier) meaning to jokes and stories. I didn't associate her with discipline or having a temper, but I was aware she was strict, and she would tell us if we'd stepped out of line. She was silly and sweet, but she was no pushover. She had a quiet toughness. Everything about her seemed steady and consistent, including that she was old.

Oldness wasn't a negative. It was just a verity I was aware of. I didn't fear or resent it. Whatever my impression of old was, either you were old or you were young, and eldership included Grandma. It had to. She *was* my measuring stick for old. As I grew up, both physically and intellectually, moving from adolescent to teenager to adult, from student to professional, Grandma stayed old. We still saw each other, but less frequently. I left Ottawa for school and then work.

I hadn't been seeing much of her this past decade. Jimmy and I had been discussing her a lot. We'd get together and be talking about all the usual things, like sports, music, our work, or the 1970s BBC soap opera *Upstairs, Downstairs*, and before long we'd be passing our thoughts about Grandma back and forth like a cigarette. She was on the cusp of ninety-two. Ninety-two! Considering that cusp, she was in incredible shape, mentally and physically. Grandma was the LeBron James of old ladies born pre-Depression.

She played golf in the summer, every Wednesday, with a group of seniors. She still actively followed professional hockey and cultural affairs and politics. She might be the only ninety-year-old in existence able to offer updated stats on the fourth-line centre for the Ottawa Senators and provide professional details about the provincial leader of the NDP.

She still loved getting outside and poking around in her flower garden. I'm not sure why, but I knew that nasturtiums (and maybe daisies) were her favourite. She was still living in her own two-storey red-brick house, the same one she'd raised her children in. She still enjoyed going for strolls around the block. I could go on and on. She had even carried the Olympic torch when it came through town. She ran with it in one hand held up over her head, waving to the crowd with the other. It's more like LeBron James is the NBA's version of Grandma.

Jimmy and I always enjoy talking about these accomplishments, her joie de vivre, and the good genes we've hopefully inherited. But this year we'd noticed a few changes. Grandma was becoming a little more forgetful. She would sometimes repeat a story. She was confusing dates and mixing up times. She would forget the odd meeting. She seemed a little more tired, taking naps most afternoons. She was, in her words, "getting dottled."

She also refused to do little things like ignore the phone or hang up on assholes, and sometimes would get caught talking to telemarketers for forty minutes at a time. She'd been scammed on the phone and at her door by dodgy salesmen and frauds. She had a hard time declining invitations to play cards, especially bridge (even though she didn't love it), or invites to lunch. She was attempting to carry on as she always had. But the world was changing at an unfair pace. Time's performance eventually becomes ineluctable.

Physically, she was still an anomaly, but she also seemed maybe an inch shorter and a little more hunched, like there were invisible weights cinched to each wrist. She couldn't be much over five feet now. Her walking pace had slowed. Against her best efforts, she might even have developed a slight limp from a sore knee. She had more sun spots on her arms, hands, and face. We agreed these changes weren't huge, but they were present. We'd noticed. At some point, Grandma had gone from old to older.

"I gotta think of something better this year, nothing practical or cheesy, just something that she'd really like," I said again, wiping some sweat from just above my nose with my index finger. Whenever I wore this sweater, my body found new places to release perspiration. "But what do you get a ninety-two-year-old? It's a question as tricky as the nature of infinity."

"I got her a painting," said Jimmy. "She's always loved art."

Oh, fuck you, Jimmy. "I asked that question rhetorically."

"Well, think about it. What do you have that you could offer?"

While I thought about this, Jimmy ordered two more beers with a nod of his head.

I finally answered when our refills arrived. "I'm curious, is the point of this to try and think of a gift I can give Grandma, or just to make me feel like shit?"

"Ideally both," said Jimmy.

"It's working."

"Really, though," he said, "the answer's easy. It's time. Just time."

"Time?" I repeated neutrally, having not yet decided if I was insulted or intrigued. I'd spent the last ten years working a variety of odd jobs, from journalism to putting up drywall. One of those years, I was forced to move home to live with my parents on their farm. For the last while I'd mostly just been writing. So I worked mainly from my apartment.

I didn't have an office to go to, or any co-workers, or work trips to go on, like Jimmy.

"I know you're working on your writing, but you can also take time off. Time that you could then spend with Grandma. No one else in the family can do that as easily. So maybe I can afford to buy her a painting, but you could spend time with her." And then, "Actually, you could take her on a trip."

That was it. That's where the whole trip thing started. One sip into our second beer.

"What?" I said.

"Seriously, you guys should go on a trip."

"Jimmy, I'm not even sure I can realistically afford that plastic tablecloth. How's a trip going to work?"

"Well, you can ask her to pay for it."

It was morally uplifting to me that I'd never considered this before — convincing the receiver of my gift to pay for it. It somehow seemed — oh, I don't know — appalling.

"So you think for my gift to my ninety-two-year-old grandma I should offer to take her on a trip. And then tell her she's paying for it?"

"Exactly. The gift isn't about the money but, like I said, the time."

"What kind of trip are we talking about?"

"Well, I don't know. You could go somewhere warm."

"Like a spring break–type thing?"

He tilted his head and narrowed his eyes. "Not exactly."

"Does Grandma even like warm?" I asked. Personally I'd always hated heat, sun, and beach vacations. With my fair skin and bony thighs that can't fill in the tightest spandex, I'm as physically suited to those trips as I am to giving birth.

"I know what you're thinking, it's you who hates the idea of going somewhere warm."

"How dare you! Don't assume."

"You could fly out to Winnipeg. She could show you around where she grew up."

"Winnipeg? You think she'd like that?" Whoa, Winnipeg! Hold on, sir! I didn't want beach, but I didn't want the complete lack of *any* warmth, either. Plus I haven't taken a trip anywhere in years, and now I've ended up in a city with one of the country's highest crime rates and the nation's largest mosquitoes? Really?

"She'd probably love it. It's you who'd hate it."

"But what about flying? Do you think she wants to go in an airplane?" I've never loved flying.

Jimmy rolled his eyes.

"Seriously, you think it would be okay, just the two of us?"

"Why not?"

"I don't know, I've never spent any time with Grandma alone before. What would we do every day? She'd be forced out of her routine."

"It's not Grandma and her routine I'd be worried about."

"I know, I know. But —"

"Stop worrying for three seconds of your life. Get out of your own head."

"But, I mean, I'm used to being alone all the time. And she'll be ninety-two!"

"Yeah, so? You're, what, twenty-eight. It would be great. You could use the company for a few days."

"Well, do ninety-two-year-olds go on trips?"

"She's old, she's not unportable."

"But she's slowing down a bit."

"She's fine. She's great."

"I know, I know."

I was thinking about the previous August. Grandma had been at a nearby mall, getting her hair done at a generic salon. She still liked to get it done every week. It was a muggy day and she'd been sitting in the stylist's chair for three-quarters of an hour. The stylist had been chatting the entire time, asking her questions and saying she couldn't believe Grandma was in her nineties. She wished her own mother was looking as good. She kept talking about her hair too, how beautifully white it was, just like snow. I'm sure Grandma was bashfully shrugging off these compliments the way I've seen her do countless times.

After she paid, she walked out into the mall. She was feeling good and, as always, liked her new cut. Several steps outside the stylists' she fell, inexplicably. When a little old lady with a head of freshly coiffed white hair falls in plain view, dropping her purse, a commotion will ensue. And it did.

That was the worst part for her. She didn't care about the fall or the sharp pain in her knee. She was embarrassed. She hated attention and fuss more than anything. Although she never mentioned it, the knee that likely caused the fall was still bothering her. It was probably getting worse.

"I think she's fully recovered," said Jimmy.

"That's what she says, but I think her knee still bothers her. You just never know, because it's physically impossible for her mouth to form a complaint."

"And that's why it'll be such a good match, because you always complain. It'll balance out on the trip."

"I don't know. I'm still thinking about that tablecloth. You really have to see it."

But by the time we'd finished our third beer, the trip was verging on becoming an interesting possibility. It was still only a possibility. But it was the *only* possibility. And as much as I didn't want to admit it, a ninety-two-year-old travelling companion was actually right in my wheelhouse. Lots of strolls, time for reading, cups of tea, ten hours of sleep per night, not too much direct sunlight, three square meals a day. It would be my kind of pace. It would be my kind of trip.

"So how are things in Kingston?" wondered Jimmy. "You doing all right these days? Anything new?"

The past few months, I've experienced a growing weariness. A tedium with where I live, with how I make a living, with my routine. I'm growing tired of my city, tired of my street, the trees, the sidewalks. I'm fatigued by the gravel covering my driveway, by the droning fridge in my apartment.

"Kingston? Oh, well, I'm fine," I said, picking up my empty glass, bringing it to my mouth before setting it back down. "Yeah, yeah, I mean, you know. I'm okay."

1:32 p.m.

IT FEELS AS if the scene has been eerily duplicated from this morning, from my street. Grandma's neighbours, a mother with two children, stroll by as we pack the car. They wave first and we reciprocate.

"Where are you off to?" the mother calls. "Looks like you're going on a trip."

"Yes, I am. With my grandson."

"Sounds like fun," she says. "I could use a trip."

One of the kids sits down on the curb. He's holding a stick in his left hand and tracing something hieroglyphic on the pavement.

"I know. I'm lucky, all right. It is going to be fun. I haven't been on a trip in a while."

Lucky? Fun? I haven't considered either of these adjectives in weeks, months. Does Grandma actually believe this, or does she just understand the socially acceptable pre-trip idiom to share with your middle-aged neighbour when your grandson is loading the car within earshot?

I'm still staring, gape-mouthed, into the trunk. I finally look up. "Oh, sorry, Grandma." She's waiting at her locked door. Grandma's even shorter than I remember. But sturdy, not frail. She's dressed sharply, with a cardinal-red collared blouse and a soft woollen shawl around her shoulders. My cut-off jeans feel more flippant than they did an hour ago.

I finally manoeuvre room for both of Grandma's bags in front of the duvet and behind the cooler. I slam down the rusty trunk and walk around to her side of the car. "There you go," I say, opening her door. "Don't worry, it's comfy. Well, comfier than it looks."

She pats my arm. "It looks cozy."

The door, like the car, is tired. It groans and sags on its greasy hinges. Grandma smiles, lowering herself gradually, carefully. She steadies herself on my left arm all the way onto the low-riding seat.

That's when I notice my front licence plate is hanging on by a single screw. The left screw is long ago lost. But, as Dad pointed out earlier, I keep it in place with grey duct tape. The most recent strips of tape must have lost their hold. I usually have to re-tape every two weeks or so. I ask Grandma to hand me the roll that I keep on the handbrake.

As I straighten and fasten the dented licence plate, my delicately positive mood disintegrates. With Grandma watching, this act makes me feel much more foolish and unsophisticated than it usually does. And realizing this, that I usually don't feel any remorse or embarrassment over continuously taping my front plate, fills me with a deep self-directed sourness.

But our endeavour is official now. It's no longer speculative. It's real. It's happening. Grandma's sitting in my car. I've swung her door shut. Even while I drove to her house, part of me still didn't believe our trip would actually happen. Maybe I'd just pick her up and she'd tell me she'd decided it'd be best not to go away for so long, and we'd go out for a nice lunch and that would be that. Then I could go home to my apartment, to my slippers. The most difficult thing for me might be having constant company for five days, the responsibility to make conversation with another person, to make meals for another person, an older person. I suppose I can cope. I'm hoping she can.

The neighbour is well down the street when Grandma confirms with a smile and nod that both her feet are inside, and I swing her door closed.

For a moment I stand back and look at my old car with my old Grandma encased inside. "So cozy," she says again from within.

1:39 p.m.

SO FAR, SO good. Our trip is off to a fine start. There have been no significant mishaps. My mood is sweetening.

Granted, we've yet to make it out of Ottawa. In fact, we're just out of Grandma's neighbourhood. Like Mom predicted, we've stopped for something to eat. I pulled out of her driveway, made a total of three turns, drove west to the outskirts of Ottawa, and she made the foreseeable suggestion. It's conceivable she heard my stomach growl. "I bet you're hungry. Do you want to stop for some lunch?"

"I could probably eat. But are you hungry?" I never know with old people. Their appetites seem constantly uncertain.

"Up to you, dear."

"I'm easy, I can always eat. This is your trip. What do you think?"

"I'm happy to stop — if that's what you want."

"Well, are you hungry, Grandma?"

"Oh, sure. I could be. And if you're hungry, then we should stop."

"How about this place?" I point at a pan-Asian restaurant to our right. I know Grandma loves Vietnamese food. She nods and grins. She's holding her purse on her lap with both hands.

There's no parking in front so Grandma directs me to

the back through a narrow alley. She's been here before. There's only one other car in the spacious rear lot. With plenty of suitable spots to select from, I coast bafflingly over to the far south side and park beside a green dumpster that smells foul. Grandma has about two feet of space to exit the car.

"You're a good parker," she comments sincerely after her escape. "It's so straight, and right between the lines."

We stand outside the restaurant, trying to decide if it's too cold for the patio. Grandma comments on the overcast sky. She thinks we could use the rain. She thinks farmers need it for their crops. I tell her it's not supposed to rain. I think the clouds will pass. Regardless, the breeze has teeth, and I'm shivering in my cotton T-shirt. I wish I had a woollen shawl, too. She scans my protruding goosebumps.

"Okay," she says, "let's go inside."

Once inside, Grandma insists I choose our table. Isn't she worried I'll pick the one beside the garbage can? I am.

I think about putting the question back to her. I'm certain she'll just deflect it back on me. So I flick my head toward a booth on our right. "How 'bout that one?"

"Good choice," she says, tossing her purse in first. "I've sat here with your mom before."

The bench is low and the table rises to just under Grandma's chin. She rests her arms on the surface. Kleenex pokes out from one of her red sleeves. Grandma points out some of the other booths she's sat in; more than half. We wait for service.

Her hands have held on to an elegant toughness. Apart from the odd liver spot or new freckle, they don't look all that different than when I was a kid. They're strong, womanly hands. They aren't delicate. These are hands acquainted with work. Her nails are strong, durable. She has them all trimmed the same length, no chips or broken edges. She wears a thin bracelet on her left wrist and two rings on the same finger — her engagement and wedding rings, I assume. I don't recall ever seeing her without these rings. It appears they have become part of her finger, embedded into the skin like the bark of an old tree.

She's helping me navigate my one-page laminated menu, pointing out options. "Their hot and sour soup is delicious," she's saying. "It's just so different."

"I think I'll get a bowl of that."

"What else?" she says.

We each decide on some soup and to split a couple of meat dishes.

"Now, what else?"

"Oh, mmm," I mumble. "Hmmm."

"Maybe we should get some spring rolls."

"Right," I say. "I always enjoy a good roll, be it egg or spring."

"Pardon?"

"Oh, just that I like spring rolls, Grandma."

"Good. And what about some fried wontons? I love those little wontons." We've just stacked our menus and, I thought, finished compiling our order. "I can never resist those crisp little wontons."

"Who can?" I say. I'm not sure I've ever tasted a wonton before. They sound vaguely familiar.

As we wait for our food, two more duos arrive for lunch.

They seem much less interested in the whole dining-out experience and more concerned with basic feeding. Neither table needs menus. Both order instantly. Two men in pastel-coloured golf shirts with black phones fastened to their black belts sit in the booth directly in front of us. They sit silently, waiting for their noodles, and unholster their phones.

I think one of the reasons Grandma fancies this place is not only the authentic fare but also the service. A short, slim Vietnamese lady in plastic sandals, who I presume is the owner, buzzes around all three tables. She moves purpose-fully, ceaselessly. The second I extract an inch of water, the plastic pitcher attached to her arm is spilling more icy liquid into my glass. She smiles and nods as she does it, as if her wide grin functions symbiotically with the flow of water. Her eyes watch me, not the glass. It's a strange dynamic, and my instinct is to simply mimic her behaviour. I grin and nod back. We grin and nod together, thanking each other. I think I've said thank you forty or so times already.

"Thank you for the water," I'm saying again. "It's very good water. Thank you."

For some reason, as I yammer on, I find the palms of my hands coming together and touching my chest like I'm praying. Thankfully, I am able to resist muttering my last florid expression of gratitude without adding a discernible Vietnamese accent.

Grandma's knowledge of Vietnamese food is reliable, especially considering she came to it so late in life. She tells me she didn't start eating it until she was in her eighties. She always loved North American–style Chinese food but now prefers both Vietnamese and Cambodian.

Our dishes arrive. As declared, the soup is pleasantly hot and sour. The chalky broth is thick, like it's holding a very fine cloud of sand. The crispy wontons are a deep-fried treat. We secured a bundle of eight with our order, and I've already devoured my four. In a resourceful display utterly devoid of dignity and etiquette, I used them as edible spoons to scoop up slippery vermicelli noodles.

This is what happens when I arrive at this level of hunger, and I don't realize I'm there until I see and smell the food. I proceed to eat like the meal is a dietary shopping spree of sorts, like I have a brief, finite amount of time to absorb as much of the plate as possible before it's taken away. It's glutinously gratifying for me but must be visually offensive for any companion or observer.

I've consumed my half of the pork dish, too, a third of the chicken dish, and my spring roll. The chicken dish contained almond halves, and I'm pretty sure I had most of them (by *pure* coincidence).

Grandma is enjoying the food but is advancing at a moderate pace. If I'm sprinting, she's crab-walking. Grandma's not yet halfway through her soup. That's it. She hasn't made a move for anything else. "It's so good, so different," she's saying, savouring each spoonful. "Better even than last time, I think. I love it here."

"Yes, it's very good, Grandma."

I set down my cutlery. I take a breath. Our table is much quieter when I stop my rapid feeding. It permits the adult-contempo' radio station a more prominent role. This is only our first meal. We'll have many more on this trip. At least three a day. For a minute I just listen to the Goo Goo Dolls and watch Grandma eventually progress to her chicken. It's possible this will be our tastiest meal of the trip. She carefully slices an already bite-sized piece of white meat into three smaller pieces. She sets her knife down carefully, impales a single microscopic morsel, and brings it slowly up to her mouth. Her hand shakes marginally. She chews and swallows.

I make a mental note to start seriously adjusting my consumption speed.

I wipe my napkin across my hot and sour lips and set it down. It absorbs some of the remaining sauce and sticks to the mostly empty plate. I take another sip of water, attempting to be sly. I don't want a refill. The owner is behind the counter; her eyes rise up. How does she know? This was a negligible sip. I don't want any more. I don't need a full glass. The sip is small enough to fit on the face of a coin without spillage. She's reaching for something — fuck — her pitcher.

"It really is very good," says Grandma.

The owner approaches, but instead of filling me up, she sits down at the adjacent table. "How you like?" she asks.

Grandma and I both answer that the food is very good. We thank her. I go a step further and say "delicious." Grandma echoes my sentiment. The owner is glad but stays where she is. Her shoulders slouch like she's uninterested in finishing her shift. I'm not sure what else to do, so I ask, "How are you doing?"

"I have bills."

Not the answer I was expecting. "Shucks," I offer.

"Very expensive here."

Grandma is blowing on a spoonful of soup.

"Oh, that's too bad. It's tough, isn't it," I say, my chin down on my chest, restraining a burgeoning burp.

"And my feet, my feet hurt." She holds one leg up off the floor. "Both my feet."

"It's not easy." I'm starting to wish she'd just refill my water.

"Lots of pain."

"Geez." I'm still peckish and am undressing one of Grandma's spring rolls with my eyes. It's still untouched. What do they put in there? Is it meat?

"The rent here too high."

"Well..." Sprouts for sure. Are the sprouts washed first?

"You know how much I pay?"

I clear my throat. "Hard to say, it's such a nice spot here...it's so roomy..."

"I pay too much," she says.

As if summoned to expand her case, a chef in customary whites surfaces from what appears to be the very depths of the kitchen. One of the other tables still doesn't have any food. They're looking concerned as they watch him abandon his post.

The chef is sweating and could either have just been working hard in a hot kitchen or have put in a few hours on a steeply inclined treadmill while wearing a garbage bag tracksuit. His face is glistening. He doesn't say anything but puts his hand on Grandma's back. There's a beige Band-Aid wrapped around his index finger. She hadn't seen him approach. It startles her. She sits up bolt-straight, bringing one hand to her chest. "Oh, hello," she says, resting her spoon on the lip of the bowl.

"You know," he says directly to Grandma, ignoring the rest of us, "you know who you remind me of?" His accent is much less pronounced than the server's; like the Band-Aid, it's hardly noticeable.

Grandma looks at me, then to the server, and finally up to the chef. She raises one eyebrow, the way she always does when pondering. "Who?"

"You. You remind me of my grandmother back in Vietnam."

"Oh, really, *me*?" says Grandma.

"Oh, yes, it's amazing." I assume his grandma back in Vietnam is likely Vietnamese. Not Scottish.

"That's nice," says Grandma.

"Yes, yes. You remind me so, so much," he repeats, keeping his hand on her back.

2:21 p.m.

GRANDMA INSISTS ON paying. I tried. I said I'd pay. She said she wanted to treat me for picking her up, and shot me her eyebrow. She doesn't use her eyebrow only when pondering but also subconsciously lifts it as a sign of authority, a facial exclamation point. It's understood by all of us in the family that when it rises, it's her little ninety-two-year-old way of visually suggesting, *Cut the crap. Do as I say.*

She gives me her credit card and asks me to go up and pay for her. I suspect the machines with tip options and PIN numbers are becoming increasingly difficult for her to navigate. She'll meet me at the car. It's okay, this is only day one.

We're starting on a trip. I'll have plenty of chances to treat her.

Back inside my car, I'm sucking on my red-striped mint. Grandma is struggling mightily with her seatbelt. The humidity and dew point in here feel analogous to those of an equatorial rainforest. I'm already buckled in. Grandma's managed to coil the twisted belt around her like a wrinkled beauty pageant sash. She's found the latch with her free hand but can't bring the metal ends together. I've stopped in the alley. I let her struggle for a moment, unsure how to help, pretending to examine the laces of my left shoe. "Oh, here, Grandma, let me try. That damn seatbelt has a mind of its own."

"No, it's okay," she's saying, bracing herself with her right hand on the door. "It's just so silly. It's my fault."

I lean over the armrest and tug forcefully on her belt. She grunts. Fuck. "I'm sorry," I say. I can feel my forehead starting to dampen. "Look," I say, "I think it's tangled up there, near the top. Let me try this." I tug harder. She grunts again, louder.

I'm up kneeling on my own seat. I need the extra leverage. My arms are stretched out in front of Grandma's face, close enough for her to bite my forearm. The car is idling. She's tilting back as far as she can, stuck to her seat like an astronaut at takeoff.

Finally I'm able to untangle the tangle. I give Grandma the okay, but still the belt needs another inch or two of line before it'll latch. Maybe it just needs a firmer pull. I try again, more firmly still. A third, more guttural grunt echoes throughout the car.

"I'm really sorry about this," says Grandma. "I know I

ate a bit too much, but I couldn't have grown this much from lunch, could I? I shouldn't have eaten so much. Sometimes I just can't resist." She's starting to laugh now. "It's from those little dandies."

"Sorry, the what?"

"Those doohickeys." I've got my right arm all the way behind her seat now and am trying to work the belt from underneath. I can't see her. "Those silly little wontons. I didn't need them but I can never resist."

She's giggling hard now; I'm fake-laughing harder. Her twitching torso is making this belt brouhaha worse. Another car has pulled up behind me. I'm getting flustered. "Why don't you just drive, I'll be fine," she says.

"We better get you buckled in, Grandma." I peer at the person behind me in the rear-view mirror. They don't look annoyed or angry, more perplexed at what's happening in the car in front of them to the little old lady with white hair.

It's when Grandma's laughing subsides that I'm able to latch the belt. "There," she exclaims, "you got it! Way to go, Iain!"

Still concerned that she can't breathe with the restrictive belt, I distractedly turn out into traffic. Grandma is still praising me. Instantly, we're almost struck. I have no idea how I didn't see the oncoming car, but I didn't. It was very close. Maybe I was still thinking about the belt, the car behind me, or the wontons. The encroaching car is able to swerve nimbly into the left lane, narrowly missing the left side of my back bumper. Grandma doesn't notice the near miss. She hears the horn blast, though. My heart is pumping.

"What's their problem? I hate those stupid horns."

"I know, eh. Just a jerk, Grandma," I say. "Clearly he has an axe to grind."

"Those people shouldn't be driving."

"You've got that right."

Arriving at the next traffic light, I timidly pull up alongside the car I almost hit. I'm still rattled by the near miss. I look through my window and through theirs. The jerk with the axe to grind is a middle-aged woman with a deflated perm. She doesn't look over at us but stares straight ahead pacifistically. She has a plastic yellow air-freshener in the shape of a foot dangling from her rear-view mirror.

What a bitch.

3:19 p.m.

THIS WASN'T PART of the grand plan. We've stopped speaking. Not for any discernible reason. We're just not talking. Silence isn't usually bad in itself, but this one is uncomfortable. Maybe it's the heavy lunch. It could be all that greasy food that's muzzled us. Or the realization that we'll be spending every minute of every day, for the next five, together. Grandma's half-whistling, half-humming meekly through her teeth. She's thinking, *Why has my grandson taken me on a trip when he has nothing to say?*

Without the distraction of chatter, my sense of smell has been heightened. I'm holding my nose high like a tentative marsupial. But I can extricate only two smells. My usual car smell: a mix of burning oil and metallic grinding.

The second, more unpleasant smell is reminiscent of lunch. I'd been anticipating a third — old lady scent. I have no idea what old lady scent is, but I was legitimately concerned. I feel like most grandmas in their nineties would either smell oddly sour or, if they resorted to perfume, too flowery, too manufactured. Grandma is determinedly scentless.

"How about a goofball, Grandma? My treat."

"What's that, dear?"

While driving, even cruising, my car gives off a tremendous groan. The muffler is long-ago shot. I have to speak up.

"A coffee. Would you like a coffee?"

"Sure. But what did you call it?"

"A goofball. I don't know why, but that's what I call coffees on road trips."

"I like that. Goofballs. Let's get some goofballs."

We pull into a Tim Hortons on the main street of Smiths Falls, a town about an hour or so northeast of Kingston. "What do you want in your goofball, Grandma?"

"Milk in my goofball, please. And here, take this."

Her hand grabs mine. My instinct is to pull away, but she forces a five-dollar bill into my squished palm with unexpected strength. I open my mouth to protest, but only muster, "Okay, be right back." I push the note into the back pocket of my jeans.

There's only a short queue, so I don't wait long. I order our drinks from a short, chinless man who is more interested in asking about my glasses than handing me our goofballs. They are ready, sitting right beside him on the counter, as we chat about the cost of prescription lenses.

The coffees are (still) steaming hot when I get back to the car. They taste good. But they do nothing to get us talking. Maybe I should have invited the employee from the coffee shop to join us. It's tricky to tell how long it's been since we last spoke. I mean, I'm focused on driving. Other than the Hank Williams tape playing, it's probably been twenty minutes or so, maybe half an hour, of obtrusive quiet. It's Grandma who finally breaks it. "Oh, the tape player still works."

"Yup," I answer, turning it up a hair. "Still sounds pretty good."

She leans forward and pats the dashboard affectionately.

"Amazing, you're still hanging in there," she says, patting the dash again. "Like me."

"Yup, it's getting up there. About twenty years old now."

"Well, I'd say that's about ninety-two in human years. The old blue bird looks pretty good considering."

I'd forgotten; that's what Grandma has always called this car. Grandma loves nicknames. The blue bird. My ninety-two-year-old car.

INSTEAD OF THE major four-lane highway, I've opted for the slower, more scenic two-lane route. We're on vacation, and efficiency isn't our aim. Unlike Highway 401, this track doesn't bypass each small town. It passes through them. The mention of the radio/tape deck seems to have uninhibited us. Grandma is speaking more freely.

"That looks like a new house. Over there, is that a new place?"

As we continue on, Grandma's interest in the local real estate swells. She mentions several more homes and asks specifically about the newness of three others. It's always too late when I look, and I can't confirm or deny their age. Although the vast majority of homes on this stretch of highway are old. "Which one?" I ask again, looking back over my shoulder.

"We've passed it now. But I didn't recognize it. There seem to be lots of revived properties on this road."

Between the new houses in the old towns, there are green meadows and brown fields. Many of both. Some are impressively manicured and await seeding. Family farms still exist in this part of the country, and evidence of their workings is scattered around the fields like children's toys — wagons and tractors, bales of hay, pickup trucks. Rusty swing sets occupy lawns. Tire swings hang from branches. Other fields are less polished. They are uneven, and instead of equipment are often shaded by groups of trees and bushes. We pass rocks and fences, streams and ponds. We've seen varying barns, the most common being the nineteenth-century log variety. There've been more farm animals than we could count — lots of cows, horses, sheep, even a donkey or two. Grandma mentions it all, reflecting aloud.

"It's so green here," Grandma says. "So green, especially for this time of year."

"You're right. It is green."

"It's quite . . . moggy." I've never heard Grandma use *moggy* before. Sometimes she has her own words or pronunciations for things. I know what she's getting at.

"Yeah, fairly."

"More here than Ottawa."

"Yes."

"There are more swamps along this road than I remember."

"I guess it is green and swampy and...moggy."

"Oh, yes." She's slanted in her seat, gazing out the window, her right hand up on the glass. "Lovely and moggy."

"Nice to still see some of these farms, too, isn't it?"

"It is, dear. I can remember when I first came out to Ontario, from the Prairies. I couldn't believe what they called farms out here. They were so small. You haven't seen farms until you see what they have in the Prairies."

"I'm sure you're right, Grandma. These are what I think of when I think of a farm." These small stone houses and scatterings of barns and wood fences. Lots of trees around. A few cattle, maybe a field of a corn. But even these farms, especially closer to Ottawa, are disappearing. "But the land is more valuable as real estate."

"Makes you wonder where we'll grow our food," she says. "These fields are so nice."

Our chatting has grown so continuous I've turned the tape down low. It was difficult for Grandma to decipher between me, the speakers, and the engine. She'd either ask me to repeat something or, more commonly, I could just tell by her void expression that she hadn't caught what was said. We've been talking mostly about the scenery around us, which has become very rocky.

"It's funny," she's saying, "we went for a lot of drives and little trips like this, but we never once went to Kingston."

"You mean you and Grandpa?"

"Yes, George loved going away."

"You guys used to take a lot of drives?"

"Oh, sure, even just for the weekend. We both enjoyed a change of scene." She's tacked her focus back inside the car.

"Did you often go away?"

"We did, yes. We were just lucky we were able to. Some of my fondest memories are the small trips we made around Ontario." I'm not sure if this announcement should make me feel more pressure to show Grandma a good time or just reinforce the notion that she enjoys this species of trip. "But," she continues, "we never went far."

"Still nice to get away."

"And I often did the driving."

"Neat." Shit. I knew it. She thinks I'm a bad driver. Maybe she wants to take over?

"Your grandpa liked to navigate and I liked doing the driving."

"I can believe that. So do you want to drive now?"

"What? No, no, dear. I'm happy to just sit here and look out there."

She sounds genuine. I guess I should just keep driving.

"Once, I remember it very well, George told me to pack up, that we were going somewhere as a surprise. I had no idea what to pack. We ended up driving five minutes away, to a motel in Bells Corners."

Bells Corners is really only a short stretch of road in western Ottawa. There are a few restaurants, some shops, and (apparently) a motel or two.

"So is that where you stayed?"

"Yup, for the whole weekend. Ten minutes from home.

47

You used to have to sign in, in an actual book in those days, when you checked in."

"Like in *Psycho*."

"And after we signed in, the guy gave us a room way at the back even though it wasn't busy." I'm not quite sure what Grandma's implying, and she must sense my momentary daze. "He read the address on the sign-in sheet and knew it wasn't far." My face is still blank, my wheels turning faster than the car's. "He assumed we were having an affair."

"Oh, right, yes, yes."

"I told my friends I'd gone to B.C. — as in Bells Corners — for the weekend, which was true." She leans toward me, grabbing my elbow. "You see, doing something like that, that was typical George."

WE'VE BEEN BEHIND the same car since our coffee stop. I think I'm following too closely. There is a small sticker of Calvin (from *Calvin and Hobbes*) above the bumper. Calvin is grimacing while urinating on an indecipherable shape, which is smaller. Both the urine spray and the secondary shape are part of the same sticker. It might just be a car logo I'm unfamiliar with. But he's definitely peeing. The car was in the Tim Hortons parking lot with us.

There are several other bumper stickers plastered around the licence plate. I can read most of them. One sticker has a sentence containing either the word *BEAST* or *BREAST* written in large, bold lettering. I can't quite make it out. I wonder if Grandma can.

I'm definitely tailgating.

I can't tell if it's a man or woman or teenager driving. I didn't see them in the lot. Now I can see only the inert head of a short figure extending a few inches above their seat. They are either alone or have a very short passenger.

I'm unfamiliar with this hamlet we're driving through. It seems like a fine place. Although maybe just a touch isolated. I don't know its inhabitants or its edicts or if they play lots of banjo music here. Just to be safe, I drop my speed down to about 75 kph, extending the asphalt void between us and the BEAST/BREAST.

TURNS OUT I didn't need to stock up at Lilac Hill. I'm glad I did, it saved me some money, but it wasn't necessary. The grocery store is open. It's Grandma who comments on the full parking lot as we cruise by. "Look at all the cars," she says. "I'd hate to be in there."

"Yeah, me too." And then I remember. I slam on the brakes, veering right into the lot. Grandma slides against her door. "Sorry, Grandma, I just have to run in and grab . . . something."

"Of course, no problem. I'll just wait here."

It takes a minute to find a spot.

"Do you want me to put the radio on . . . or another tape?" I'm pretty sure the only other tape I currently have in the glovebox is Digital Underground.

"No, dear. I'm fine just as is."

The parking lot wasn't lying. The store is bustling. I don't want to be here. But I need to be. Grandma's comment about people stocking up somehow brought to mind my lack of toilet paper. I'm fresh out. I believe I have a couple rolls of paper towel around, but with Grandma staying over, battling this congested store is a must.

I canter past the carts, through the produce aisles, the deli, the bakery, and on toward the row of tissues. People are milling about obtusely. The mood is tense. The impression is that this store, and all others, has been closed for a month or so. I'm finding it tricky to repel this stress stew.

I grab an eight-pack in front of an indecisive woman leaning in close to read the price per weight. I'm assuming Grandma is fine with mere two-ply. Three just seems overkill; four is borderline unethical. Also, two is the cheapest.

When I walk through a checkout with broccoli florets, no definitive assumption can be made. Maybe I'm making soup or will be stuffing a chicken breast. Both are likely possibilities. Even an omelet or a salad are in play. I make a broccoli and walnut salad that would bring you to your knees. But with these rolls of white TP wrapped in plastic, there's no uncertainty. Everyone I pass can see and judge my motivation as easily as my brand of shoes.

There's also an uncomfortable intimacy when handing it to the cashier. It's mildly worse when it's a female. "Do you want me to bag this?" she'll ask. She'll handle the package reluctantly, like it's infected. She'll be asking about how I want to pay but will be thinking, *My God, you revolt me... I know what you're planning on doing with these rolls when you get home. You're a disgusting, sick man!*

The guy in front of me in line can't see what I'm holding. Nor does he care. I've intuited that he's selfish. I haven't officially counted, but he has at least twelve items with him.

Make it thirteen. This is THE EXPRESS LANE!! Eight to ten items max! Three bell peppers are three items. Not one!

All the other lines look gracefully aerodynamic. They're flowing efficiently. People in those lines are smiling. I'm never lucky with picking the fastest queue. The guy in front of me is just standing there, one hand in his pocket, bouncing on the balls of his feet, as if this is his first time taking too much food through this line. He needs to be told, taught a lesson.

"Shit!" I say loudly, like I'm talking to the cashier two or three rows over. My voice is aimed squarely at his freckled bald spot. "That's my phone."

I fish my phone out of my pocket and pretend to read a number from the blank display. The battery has been dead for more than a day. I consider the fake number and hold it up to my ear. "Hey, man. No, no, not yet. I'm still at the grocery store. I know, eh. Yes, Grandma is with me. Yes. Grandma. Yeah, she's with me, all right. Yeah, but she's STILL IN THE CAR, so. Well, I thought it was going to be a very quick stop, but..."

No reaction.

"Uh, well, she's ninety-two."

Nothing, not even a look over his shoulder.

"Yeah, she's ninety-two, getting close to ninety-three. I know, eh. Yeah, she's ALONE out there. Oh, well, I cracked the window a bit."

My eyes are locked on his foul head. All I want is a look of reparation, that's it. I don't even care anymore if he stays in the line. A glance is all. Just look at me!

But it never happens. His food is swiped and bagged. He

pays with his credit card. He walks away pushing his cart, oblivious, good mood intact. I drop my dead phone back into my pocket without saying goodbye. I think my lower back is getting sore.

"WELL, THAT WAS quick," says Grandma, looking up at me.

I sit with the package of toilet paper on my lap. "Sorry about that, Grandma."

"Why? It was so interesting out here."

"In the car?"

"I've been watching people and that thing." I follow her eyes to the other side of the parking lot. "Whatever that is over there? A seagull, I think." I have to squint to see the gull. It doesn't look entirely gull-like. "He's been walking around in little circles. There must be some food for him."

"I'm not sure why people still feed those birds. It attracts more, and it's not even good for them." I'm content to continue talking about the hungry fowl that might actually be a plastic bag. I'm stalling. I have good news and bad news for Grandma. I better tell her the bad news first. "So, Grandma, I should tell you now." I inhale through my nose. "This is the trip." I look out the windshield.

"Of course it is, I'm so excited. I've been telling my friends for weeks. They can't believe it."

"No," I say, pushing the package between us into the backseat. "I mean, like, this is as far as we're going."

"You mean here in Kingston?"

I hear myself clearing my throat. "Yeah."

"Oh." She looks out her window, back toward the grocery store, and then back to me.

"We're just going to stay here...in Kingston...at my place."

"We are? Well, I think that's wonderful, dear."

No, it's not.

"But I promise we'll still do stuff. I just couldn't really think of anywhere to go and I thought or, you know, I hope it might be relaxing for you. And it's going to be my treat." And most importantly: I'm a terrible, terrible grandson and person. I'd promised you a trip. A real trip.

"Of course it will. It'll be great, better than going away somewhere far. This will be great. Isn't it called a 'staycation'?"

"I think so."

"It's going to be so relaxing for me," she says. "I'm feeling less tired already. And it's a change of scene for me. That's always a good thing."

I sag over the wheel and turn on the engine. I've decided I don't need to bother with the good news; she's already seen the new package of toilet paper.

5:11 p.m.

IN MY GRAVEL driveway, I help Grandma out of the car and collect her bags from the trunk. I'm discouraged to see that the tape on my licence plate hasn't held. I also don't see any point in re-taping.

It feels a degree or two warmer in Kingston than it did in Ottawa. Grandma walks over to the front stairs gingerly, her knee stiff from the drive. "Do you need a hand? You look stiff."

It's Grandma who asks the question over her shoulder. To me.

"No, no, I'm fine. But what about you?"

"No, dear, I'm fine."

I follow behind, step by step, bags in my left hand. At the door I drop the cases and root around in my pockets for the key. The outside steps could use a fresh paint job, I think. Grandma puts a hand out and instinctively tries the metal handle. The door slips open. "Here we are," she says, stepping through the unlocked door. The key is presumably on my desk somewhere. I hope.

Inside there's a tiny, frayed blue carpet sitting atop blue tile. We both stand on the mat like it's an island. There's a bench built into the wall to our right. Further ahead is the kitchen. It has the most windows of any room, so it's where I hope we can spend the bulk of our time. In the other direction, the sitting area and bedrooms.

I leave Grandma on the mat and squeeze out of my tied shoes, stepping on each heel. Grandma removes hers conscientiously, one at a time. They are laced Hush Puppies, and I'm amazed to see she remains standing, bending down to undo and remove them. I push both pairs under the bench.

I walk Grandma to her room in our sock feet. She comments on any art or photos she sees on the walls, stopping to look at each one. I put her bags on the wicker chair beside her single bed. I leave her in her room to unpack. I tell her there's no rush, I'll be in the kitchen.

When Grandma returns to the kitchen about a half-hour

later, she's wearing a pair of soft slippers that look like ballerina shoes. I'm finishing up the dishes I'd left in the sink.

"It's so nice to be here," she says. "I couldn't resist trying out the bed. It's very comfy."

"It is? Well" — I dry my hands on the tea towel and sling it over my shoulder — "good. Now, how about a glass of something?"

"Oh, well, I can't say no to that. Not when I'm on a trip."

"Me neither. And I happen to have some sherry."

I tell Grandma I have the good stuff and fish my water bottle out of the cooler. I don't have any proper sherry glasses, but in their place I use some Milwaukee Brewers coffee mugs. I pour us each a few fingers. I think this is my very first sherry. We touch mugs.

As we sip, I'm picturing the face of Abraham Lincoln. I just finished reading a biography of Lincoln last night. I can see the deep lines, creases, and dark circles under his famously tired eyes. It's a long, bony face. And hairy: no mustache, but an untrimmed chinstrap. Maybe more than anyone's, I'm thinking, Grandma's face is diametrically disparate to Lincoln's. She doesn't have *any* wrinkles. She's ninety-two!! Where he has lines, she has brown freckles. Where his cheeks sink in, hers lie straight. His complexion is dark, hers fair. Where Lincoln's mane is a dishevelled brown and falls in unkempt waves, Grandma's is blank-page white, washed, and neatly combed up off her forehead. Lincoln was six four and rake thin. Grandma can't be over five feet and is healthily plump.

The sherry has done its job, converting her to talkative mode. I was hoping she would be chatty, since we're going to have lots of time for it. But I've had to ask her directly about her own memories. She's started telling me a little about her birthplace in northern Scotland, just before the 1920s.

"It was my grandmother who inherited a store on the main street in Wick."

"I didn't know your grandma owned her own store."

"Yes, but not at first. In those days in Scotland she wasn't legally permitted to own property."

"Really?"

"No, women couldn't own property. But in her mind it was her store regardless."

"What did she do?"

"She got her brother to sign the paperwork. But she was going to run it." Grandma brings her sherry up to her mouth but speaks again before drinking. "That's the whole thing, it was rightfully hers."

"That's pretty cool." It's hard to imagine something like that. It seems absurd to someone my age. But that *actually* happened in her lifetime, or just before it, anyway. Women were not allowed to own property. Also hard to imagine: that I'm drinking *and* enjoying a glass of sherry.

"And that's where I was born."

"In Wick?"

"Yes, but I mean in her store."

"You were born in the store?"

"In the apartment upstairs." She finally draws her overdue sip. "That's where we lived. My father worked at a local bakery. He was the baker. But my mother worked, too. She took over the store after my grandmother died. She ran it."

"That must have been rare in those days, for a mother to be working."

"It was, I suppose, yes," she says thoughtfully.

I'M BACK OVER at the cooler, pawing around like a raccoon. I should have put the food away already. The bag of ice cubes is a bag of cold water. I'm getting hungry again. "So what do you feel like for supper, Grandma?"

"I was thinking maybe we should go out. Since it's the first night of the trip. It should be something special, I think."

"Are you sure?" I ask, exhibiting a room-temperature ball of semi-thawed lamb meat from the cooler. "We could always stay here."

"I'd be happy to go out. What do you think?"

"Sure, why not? But I should probably put this stuff away first."

"Okay, I'll just wait here."

But before I even reach the fridge, Grandma is up from her chair. "Actually, I'll be right back." She walks over to her purse, which she's left sitting by the door, and slings it over her shoulder. "Just give me a minute."

The cooler is empty when she walks back into the kitchen five minutes later. I'm flipping through the last section of the newspaper. I look up. Grandma has changed.

She's wearing different slacks (her word) and a different, fancier blouse. She's pinned a silver brooch to the left lapel. She has a soft silk scarf tied around her neck. Her hair has been retouched in the front. It's pushed back, higher, and looks airier. She's readied herself to dine out. It's all intensely endearing.

"We're going out," she says, "and it's a silly habit I can't break. I just had to put on a little lipstick."

It's true. She's also wearing a fresh coat of maroon lipstick.

7:53 p.m.

IT'S BEEN A day of extremes. Either it's been just the two of us — in the car, at my place — or it's been busy: the Tim Hortons, the grocery store, and now the restaurant. The hostess shows us to a table set for three, next to a window with a view of Ontario Street. Grandma hangs her purse on the back of her chair as the hostess clears the third setting.

"This is nice," says Grandma. "It smells so good in here. I'm hungrier than I thought. I shouldn't have been talking so much before dinner; it made us late."

"We're not late. I always eat around this time." With the music and background chatter, it's loud. I'm concerned it's too loud for Grandma. "Are you sure this is okay?"

"It's lovely," she says. "Great atmosphere in here. Nice to see all the young people."

The hostess has been supplanted by an older waitress who introduces herself, drops two glasses of water on the table, along with two menus, and asks if we want anything to drink.

"Maybe just give us a second or two," I say.

"Aren't you going to get some wine?" wonders Grandma.

The waitress, a step away, freezes and then looks back over her shoulder.

"Oh, well, yes, I could probably have a glass. Are you going to have any?"

"No, dear, I'm fine." She turns to the waitress. "One glass of..." and then back to me.

"Red, I think. House red is fine."

The waitress nods and retreats. We can see the exposed kitchen from our table, a wood-burning oven and the tall chef tossing his pizza dough into the air. With a quick pan, I discern that the uniform for this place is tight and black. The majority of servers are stereotypically attractive females: lots of exposed tanned flesh and tight blond ponytails.

I hand one menu to Grandma. We've reversed our roles from lunch. Since I've been to this restaurant and Grandma hasn't, I'm helping her make a decision. I don't often eat at restaurants, but this is one of the busiest in Kingston. They specialize in gourmet pizza but have an inclusive menu of chicken, fish, salads, even wild boar.

"We could always just split a couple of things, that could be good."

"Yes, of course," she says.

"They have good pizza here. Could you eat some pizza?"

"Of course." She puts down her menu. "Whatever you think."

"Okay, and what about sharing an appetizer to go with it?"

"Of course."

"These sound good." I reach over and retrieve her menu, planting my index finger next to the blackened chicken spring rolls with feta. Grandma squints at the selection. It's not just noisy in here but dark, too. The candles on the tables are the main source of light. I read the description to her.

"Yup, sounds good," she says. "I absolutely love feta."

After we place our order, I sip my wine. Grandma does the same with her ice water. I'm aware that people are intrigued by us, almost goggling. Grandma is also *au courant* with their looks. "It's my white hair." She winks. "They're all surprised to see me out so late."

Grandma and I have been together for about eight or nine hours. We've shared two meals. We've drunk some coffee, some sherry, and some wine. Nothing disastrous has happened. We still have four more days of this trip to endure. I have no idea what else we can do. What else can we do?

Seriously. Showing a ninety-two-year-old a good time, or a mediocre time, or just *a* time, is going to be harder than I thought. I fear an imminent lack of interest, of fun. Just a few days ago I called a friend to see if he had any ideas for me, tips on how to inject some carefree mirth into the trip. He reminded me that I wasn't really the fun or adventurous one in our group. He didn't really think that was my nature. He thought it best for me to be myself. When pushed for which one in the group I was, he used the word *egghead* and asked what the opposite of an adrenaline junkie was. I wonder if I can offer Grandma a sherry first thing tomorrow morning?

Since picking her up today, I've been thinking more about my own earlier life. It's a reaction I wasn't anticipating. Her reminiscences have made me introspective, more even than usual. I've been in Kingston, this small town, and living in my apartment for a couple of years now. I don't spend much time reminiscing or chatting or telling old stories or sharing memories of earlier years. I mostly work from home. I don't know many people in Kingston. I'm often alone. I imagine Grandma's life at the same age was much different.

It's raining now. It must have just started, but puddles are starting to form. Grandma is nibbling her first bite of pizza contentedly. She eats like a bird, with tiny, careful bites. She nods to show she likes it. I take a bite and look out the window again. Even though it wasn't forecast and I didn't want to admit it, I knew it was coming. Everything about today had rain written all over it.

TUESDAY

8:14 a.m.

IT'S HARD TO wake up. It's always a challenge for me to shake the fog of sleep. Today is especially onerous. I'm lying on my side in a makeshift fetal position, using one pillow between my knees as the filling of a leg sandwich. A second pillow has fallen to the floor somewhere (my left arm is substituting unsuccessfully for it). I'm squinting at the wall, listening to the alarm's abhorrent beeping. I don't always set an alarm. I make my own work hours. Sometimes I work late at night. My typical morning commute is the several feet over to my desk.

But I'm currently responsible for a ninety-two-year-old. This week is an alarm week.

It's stayed so pleasantly dark in my room this morning; cave-like, in a good way. It's how I prefer it. What normally feels too small and cramped during the day is currently a snuggery. I left my window open, only an inch. It's filled my room with a tepid briskness only available in this part of early spring. And it's acting as a natural sedative. With the help of a sheet and blanket, we (the room and I) have hit the optimal sleeping conditions.

I roll over and reach to switch off the alarm, and then fall onto my back with my arms and legs spread. There's more, higher-pitched beeping. Somewhere in the world, a large truck is reversing. People have started their day. People are eating breakfast and taking their kids to school. People are interacting. People are working and contributing to society. People are driving trucks in reverse. I should get up.

I swing my legs out and scratch the back of my head. I stand and stretch, pushing my fists into my lower spine. Without my quilt I feel cold. I feel naked. I see my reflection in the mirror to my left. I am naked.

The room has suddenly swapped its Spring Freshness for Fucking Coldness. I collapse inward like a folding lawn chair, bringing my arms into my core. My first job is to locate my robe and my shorts. I do so triumphantly, and grab some socks off the floor, and sit down at my desk.

I scribbled a few notes last night describing some stories Grandma told me. She was in a reminiscent mood throughout supper and dessert. I hadn't heard them before, and although spotty, they were captivating. I find it easy to forget how long she's actually lived. I tried to get more details from her, but those are the areas that seem to have crumbled first. Like a Victorian stone wall, it's the in-between fastening material, the concrete that starts to fragment, while the stones stay moderately in place. There's a lot she remembers. There's a lot she forgets. I'm hoping there's still more she'll tell me.

While my notebook was out, I also started a journal of ideas regarding what Grandma and I can do today. I review it now while my computer and I warm up. I read it once and turn it over, hoping to find more ideas on the back of the page. It's blank. There's nothing on this list for a rainy day.

There are a few points about walking around downtown or driving west to the town of Picton. I've reminded myself in terrible penmanship that Picton has some lovely vineyards; we could sample some wine. There's also a beach in Picton. The last line of my list: *We could go for a short walk ON THE SAND!!*

I rip out this useless page of notes, crumple it, and drop it into my wastebasket like an orange peel. My penmanship really is alarming. I always just assumed it would get better, the way I knew I would grow taller. But it never happened. Now I'm a tall man with the handwriting of an eight-year-old boy.

Of course I still don't have any hot water. I tracked down the appropriate fellow on the phone yesterday before leaving to pick up Grandma. The earliest he can come is tomorrow. Not to worry — if Grandma really needs a wash, I'm sure she won't mind soup-ladling some lukewarm kettle water over herself while leaning over the bathtub. Either that or we could both just stand outside under the rain in our bathing suits and hand a bar of soap back and forth.

That would also give us something to do today. It would kill at least twenty minutes.

Then again, maybe the rain will stop by the afternoon and we'll have time to drive to Picton and those vineyards, to the beach and the sand. For now, I can hear the rain falling relentlessly on the driveway outside my window. It sounds unending and remorseless. It sounds bored.

★

I'VE BEEN KNOCKING about the kitchen for ten minutes, maybe fifteen, the way I always am, putting dishes away, grinding coffee beans, when Grandma shuffles in. She's wearing her thin pink slippers. This is what I was most concerned about: the mornings. For people who live on their own, every form of human interaction is amplified in the morning.

I've noticed that Grandma enters rooms almost silently. After spending a day or two with most people, I can recognize their blunt footsteps as easily as their face or voice. And it irritates me. Most drag their feet or drop them inattentively. Grandma doesn't step so much as glide around. She skates. She floats.

I'm clad in my customary basketball shorts, undershirt, and housecoat. Grandma's already meticulously dressed. You'd think she was expecting company. She has that same brooch clipped to a voguish charcoal sweater. Her hair is neatly combed (of course). I look down at my frayed housecoat. The last time a comb or brush of any kind made contact with my hair, people were still smoking on airplanes.

The only evidence of recent slumber is her hardly-puffy eyes. Everything about my fish-eyed, bloated reflection in the metal kettle — the stubble, the dark circles under my eyes, the morning horns — screams that I just woke up.

"Good morning, Grandma!" I finally say, pushing the start button on the coffee maker. I've waited until she was present. I want her to know it's a fresh batch. I'm trying to sound as friendly and warm and awake and welcoming and cheery and dashing and happy and excited and all-American-grandsony as possible. I'm not used to employing my vocal cords first thing.

"Well, good morning!" she answers. Like her face, Grandma's voice carries none of the baggage of sleep the way mine does. "Still looks a little wet out there today, doesn't it?"

"Yeah. Bit of a shame, really," I say, clearing my throat for the third or fourth time.

"And how did you sleep?"

"Pretty good, I guess. Not bad. How about you?"

"Do you even have to ask?" she answers. "I always sleep well, no matter what. I'm lucky that way."

I smile. She smiles back. It's true. I've never once heard Grandma complain of a bad night's sleep, regardless of churning thoughts, environmental conditions, or sleeping quarters. Ever. My sleeping habits have improved in recent years but are still erratic. When I lived in Toronto and was working a variety of part-time jobs, I'd go weeks without having a full night's sleep. I was tired but wasn't clear how I fit into the city and felt adventively confined. On the worst nights, I'd get out of bed, leave my apartment, and go for long walks through the city, up and down Parliament Street or along Queen, regardless of weather or time of night. I don't take too many late-night walks anymore. Now when I can't sleep, I make a snack or read, or just stay lying in the dark, thinking. Even the most vapid, petty cognitional involution makes sleep unviable. Grandma moves over to the sink. She must want a glass of water! I instinctively step in front of her like a bouncer. This (understandably) startles her.

"Oh, sorry, Grandma. Do you want some water or something?" I've adapted my voice again now, to try and sound soft and hospitable. "I can get that for you, just take a seat." It's coming out sounding higher-pitched and vaguely feminine. I am a tired Canadian Truman Capote.

"Oh, well." She points at the tap, within arm's reach. "I mean, I can get it."

I wrestle my lips into another smile. "No, no, I'll do that. You just sit down."

"Okay, sure. Thanks. Well, aren't I lucky?"

She seats herself at the table. It's not just me. She's not used to this either, trying to construct canny discourse first thing in the morning. She's also not accustomed to people waiting on her. I'm certainly not used to waiting on people. We are two familiar people interacting capriciously. Grandma picks up the *Kingston Whig-Standard* I've brought in from the front stoop. The coffee maker drips and hisses.

"I just love the Kingston paper," she says. "I like reading about where I am."

"Yeah, they do have lots of local coverage, don't they?" I look up and to the left, nodding. I want her to think I'm really, really, really considering all the local coverage.

Grandma's also brought her own paper, the *Globe and Mail*, from home. She sets it down on the table and removes her glasses from their soft leather case. It must be yesterday's paper. She wouldn't have had the chance to read it. I think I remember her telling me once that she never likes to miss the paper, not even for a day. She likes to know what's going on.

Once the water is pleasantly cold, I lean down and

drink a mouthful straight from the tap. Then I fill her cup. Grandma accepts it and takes a wee pull. "Good water," she says, nodding her approval. But she curls her lips around her teeth the way you do when it's too cold. Grandma takes another sip, bigger this time. "Yes, quite tasty."

"It really is good water, isn't it?" I thought everybody liked water ice cold?

"It certainly is."

"It's funny," I say, laughing a little louder than I need to, "I've always thought that about Kingston city water. It's quality water. I'm glad you think so, too. Although I hear they have a bit of a blue-green algae issue. Nasty stuff, that."

Blue-green algae?

The kitchen is quiet again, apart from the screeching coffee maker. I smile. Why isn't it done yet? It never takes this long, does it? I look at the digital clock on the oven. We've been together now for nearly twenty-four hours. The longest stretch I've ever been one-on-one with my grandma. Surely I have more to say to her than my endorsement of city-regulated tap water and the "good" stories in our newspaper.

"Mmmmm," she says. "Delicious."

More quiet.

"So," I blurt, eyeing the newspaper, jumping into it like a conversational lifeboat, "what's going on in the world, Grandma?"

"I'm not sure, dear." She picks it up. "Let's see."

I stand again, neurotically, to check on the coffee. She must have been only a few sentences into the top story before resting the paper back down. "You know what happens more, now that I'm old?" she says. "I see things at night, in bed. It happened again last night."

"What do you mean?"

"I see things when I close my eyes. It's never for long, because I always fall asleep so quickly. But for a little while I just see things, colours. I'm not sure how else to explain it. It's just images and colours and movement."

"That sounds odd."

"I love it," she says.

"I've never experienced that, even though I frequently dream."

"Did you dream at all last night?" she asks.

I can't recall the last time I've fallen asleep quickly or the last time I've been asked about my dreams. People aren't usually interested in the dreams of others. I walk over, handing her a cup of coffee as I answer. Now she has something cold and something hot. One for each hand. "Yeah, I think so, I usually do. But I don't remember about what. I wish I could. I almost never can remember. Did you?"

"I did dream, yes, all night. Mostly boring stuff you wouldn't care about."

"Really?" My first sip is life-restoringly good.

"One was very strange. I think I've had only about three nightmares in my entire life. But last night was very close to a nightmare." I collect my mug, pull out my chair, and sit down at the table with her again. I take a sip before answering. I do make great coffee. I wonder if she can perceive the quality of the coffee I produce?

"That sucks, Grandma. What kind of nightmare are we talking about?"

"It was very odd. I just remember falling. I was falling and it just seemed to go on and on. I don't even remember the story, or plot, or what have you. I don't even know what the point was or why my mind was set on this image of just falling and falling. It's strange, isn't it?"

"Sounds awful." Unlike this perfectly brewed coffee, which is outstanding.

"It wasn't as bad as I'm making it sound. It was still just a dream, and I always enjoyed dreaming. I still do. Even when it's not a nice dream. I think it's still good for me to be dreaming."

As we chain-sip, I wonder if dreaming, like most things, is dulled by age. Do dreams, like taste buds, lose some of their authority over time? Do our dreaming legs atrophy? Is that why an especially vivid dream, like last night's, really resonates with Grandma? It seems logical.

She continues, "Even if I'm just falling, or it's a weird dream, or nonsense, I really do still believe it's good for me. It must be good for us."

When you get closer to death, do dreams change? I wonder if dreaming about falling is in some way a metaphor for encroaching death? Is Grandma worried about dying, or is that too obvious? Or, I don't know, maybe dreams sharpen with age. Maybe they grow more vivid and carry more emotional weight. Maybe *because* our bodies age and break down, dreams are more prevailing and, in this sense, theoretically freeing. Maybe dreams are more like a blue cheese that sharpens with age. Speaking of cheese . . .

"How about a little breakfast?" I ask. "Maybe some food will help us remember a bit more of our dreams."

"Whenever you want it, dear." She picks up the paper again but looks straight ahead, past it. "It really was strange though, just falling without stop," she says. "I wonder what it all means."

IT'S MEANT TO be a sliced loaf, and was at an earlier time. It's managed to freeze itself back into an unsliced loaf. Regardless, it's our best option for breakfast this morning. Toasted, with some form of condiment. I have to use a butter knife to pry the hard pieces apart. It's been in my freezer for a couple of weeks, a month at most. "Shouldn't be much longer, Grandma," I call from the freezer. "We're almost ready."

"Okay, dear."

I drop the slices into the toaster and secure the knob of cheddar from yesterday's stolen cargo. I bring it over to the table with a dollop of firm butter and a jar of peanut butter.

"This'll do, eh, Grandma?" I pat her jockishly on the back.

She looks at the food and then at me and grins. "Looks great. I just love cheese. I often don't eat any breakfast at all, so this'll be a treat. Now, what can I do to help?"

She loves food and meals. The thought of Grandma not eating breakfast is heartbreaking.

"Nothing, we're almost ready. Just waiting on the toast."

"Well, then, I'll do the dishes when we're done," she says.

When the toast pops, I put it on a communal plate lined with a paper towel. I let Grandma choose first.

"Thanks," she says. "You know, my friends just couldn't believe this, they really couldn't."

"What do you mean?" I'm manhandling the jar of peanut butter while Grandma slices off a single serving of cheese.

"They just thought it was great I was going away, and especially with my grandson. None of them had ever done anything like it before."

I wonder what *my* friends would think of this vacation. I have an idea of what they would think. That's why I haven't told anyone about it. "Did they know where you were going, or just that I was taking you somewhere?" I take a bite, careful not to get any peanut butter on my fingers.

"Well, they knew I was off on a trip with my grandson and were just impressed by that."

She means well, but I don't enjoy being reminded of our situation. I generally adore peanut butter and have spent chunks of my life subsisting on the stuff. But as Grandma tells me how her friends are impressed by my trip plan and how they claim to be envious of her being whisked away on an extended vacation, this familiar breakfast takes on a more repugnant flavour. I'm chewing brown, oily glue.

"That's nice," I say, barely getting it down. It's looking more and more like this whole thing is misguided. Not a terrible tragedy, but certainly an avoidable blooper. How could I have done this? I've brought a very old lady out of her own warm, comfortable home, away from what she knows, out into the rain, with no hot water. And frozen bread. Why? So we can sit quietly and listen to the coffee maker?

I curse my brother under my breath.

"Pardon?" says Grandma, resting her toast on her plate.

"Oh, nothing," I say.

Grandma must detect my sudden surge of disappointment and regret. "Oh, you can have some of this cheese if that's no good."

"No, no, it's not really the food, Grandma," I answer. "I guess I just wish it wasn't raining."

Grandma, now stuck on the notion of disagreeable food, ignores my weather complaint and continues brightly. "You know, it's lucky, I guess, but I can really only remember a few times when I really couldn't eat something."

"Oh yeah?"

"Once, when I was still studying, they tried to serve us heart for lunch." She raises one eyebrow. "Can you believe that? Heart!"

"Heart, you mean like ... heart. As in heart-heart, like the organ?"

"Yes, I think probably beef heart. And the funny thing is I've always liked most organ meat. I love pâtés and head cheese." My peanut butter is starting to taste better again.

"What did you do?"

"Well, of course, I refused. And the last time I had gout the doctor told me I shouldn't be eating any organ meat at all."

"No organ meat, eh? Huh."

"I can remember getting gout for the first time when we were all on a road trip. Do you remember? You were there."

"I think so."

This has happened a few times. Grandma will start by telling me a story about one thing, which will lead to another and then another. Bad food — to heart — to gout.

"I didn't even want anyone to come near the bed. Especially you kids. I didn't say anything, but it was sore. All you guys were running in and out of the room."

We smile at the memory and finish the rest of our breakfast in reflective silence.

Once finished, we move to the sink. I'm washing and complaining about the rain. Grandma is drying. She is less discouraged. "Don't worry about the rain. There's really nothing we can do about it," she says. "I don't mind it at all. It's relaxing."

"It's not so bad, I guess. But it puts a dent in our plans for today, that's all."

"It doesn't have to," she says, holding a dripping plate with both hands.

"How so?"

"You know what would be a real treat?"

"What?" I say, looking through the wet window in front of me. It's covered in silver varicose veins of water. "We can do whatever you want."

"I'd love to just go find a chair . . . and read."

"Really?"

"Yes, dear. I don't get the chance to do that very much at home. I'd just love that."

"But that's not really a trip thing, is it?"

"Of course it's a trip thing. And today, with all the rain, it's the perfect day for it."

"Well, I guess, if you'd enjoy that."

"Oh, sure. It would be very pleasant. If you don't mind."

I take the damp towel from Grandma and hang it on the oven's handle. I lead her into the living room, to the smallish and old and pink chair. I rarely sit in it, because it's too small for me. And it's old. And it's pink.

"Lovely," she says.

I bring the side table over beside her, grab an extra pillow, turn the table lamp on, and pull up the footstool. "You're all set," I say. "You're sure you're okay with this?"

"Yes, yes. Now you go and do what you have to do. I can stay here alone." She slowly seats herself with an unwinding sigh. She stretches and lifts her legs out in front of her.

"No, Grandma, I have nowhere to be. I mean, this is what I'm doing. We're on a trip."

"Well, I don't mind. You can do some work if you have that to do."

"Well, I guess I could do some writing."

"Great, you head off. I'll be here enjoying the rain." She leans back in her chair, clasping her hands on her stomach.

"If you're sure."

So I do. I leave Grandma to read. Alone.

MY ROOM FEELS better for sleeping than anything else. I must fight the urge to crawl back into my unmade bed. And I mean, really, would that be so wrong? Grandma *told* me to go ahead and use this time as I see fit. She only *suggested* I could do some work. Besides, we're both on vacation, right?

I force myself to at least sit in front of my computer. It's understood I won't be doing much writing. I open a new web browser. For some reason I type in "1917" and hit return. It's the year Grandma was born. I'm not looking for anything in particular. The first link is the Wikipedia entry for the year.

I click on it.

"1917 (MCMXVII) was a common year starting on Monday of the Gregorian calendar (or a common year starting on Sunday of the 13-day-slower Julian calendar)."

I scroll down and read over some of the notable events of 1917: The University of Oregon defeats the University of Pennsylvania in the third annual Rose Bowl. The National Hockey League is formed to replace the National Hockey Association. Two freighters collide in Halifax Harbour and cause a massive explosion. J. R. R. Tolkien starts writing *The Book of Lost Tales* and thus about Middle-earth for the first time. The very first Pulitzer Prizes are awarded. The first ever International Women's Day is observed in Russia (she would like that). The Russian Revolution begins with the overthrow of the tsar. The independence of Poland is recognized. U.S. President Woodrow Wilson announces the end of diplomatic ties with Germany. The United States declares war on Germany. Conscription begins in the United States. After months of brutal fighting, Canadian forces take hold of Passchendaele in Belgium. Canadian troops win the Battle of Vimy Ridge.

In 1917 Vera Lynn is born. So are Ella Fitzgerald, Dizzy Gillespie, Dean Martin, and John F. Kennedy.

Both Tom Thomson and Edgar Degas die.

All that happened the year she was born. Now she's sitting in the little pink chair.

I close the window and shut off my computer. I open my desk drawer. It's filled with papers, pens, a pencil, coins, bookmarks, paperclips, a pair of earbuds, a calculator. I open it the rest of the way. More stuff. There's a recipe from the paper for a baked halibut dish I've never made. I move some envelopes around at the back and find some elastic bands. I shouldn't be wasting my time. I should be planning our afternoon, or making sure Grandma has everything she needs, or at least hanging out with her. From my desk, my bed looks so comfortable. I take one elastic from the drawer and slip it over my wrist like a bracelet.

I walk over and fall onto the mattress face first. I'll just nap for a bit.

1:18 p.m.

"I CAN'T REMEMBER for sure," I'm saying, "but I'm almost certain I was wearing my pajamas, my crimson blazer, and my moccasin slippers. This was more or less my uniform in those years."

"How old were you?"

"Around six. And on this night I was probably also wearing a tiny silk scarf around my neck, cravat-style. I had this Chopin tape I loved and I bet it was playing, too. It was around spring of '87 and I was supposed to be going to my first ever sleepover. It was scheduled for the next night. I can remember brooding, heavily."

I'm standing over the oven. Grandma is at the table. After my nap I summoned Grandma back to the kitchen for lunch. I'm wearing the NASA apron Jimmy brought me after one of his work trips to Houston. Jimmy's an engineer and spends time working at NASA whenever there is a shuttle launch. The company he works for built a laser camera system for the shuttle. On the apron is the NASA logo and the caption *I need my space.* There's no real reason why I should be wearing it. I'm not doing any cooking, but it adds to the illusion that I am, that I didn't just open a can of pea soup.

The soup is starting to bubble in the middle. I hope Grandma likes it hot. "Soup's almost ready," I say, "hang in there."

"I can't wait," she says. "So what were you brooding about?"

"I know, parties aren't something most people brood about. It wasn't really a full party. Just a couple friends, my buddies, John and Felix. I wasn't worrying about anything concrete, of course. There were just so many variables to contemplate and plug into the equation. I couldn't decide if attending a sleepover was worth it. It seemed crazy to me — why would anyone choose to leave the comfort of their own bed, their stuffed animal collection, and their clean bathroom? It was ludicrous."

I look down at the thick, salty canned soup I'm carrying over to the table — also ludicrous. At least I've included some fruit. I've peeled a banana for us to share. It's unduly ripe.

"Dig in, Grandma," I say.

"Looks good," she says. She hand-irons her napkin across her lap and blows softly on her first spoonful. One mouthful in, she opts to rest her spoon on the bowl. She's never in a rush.

Investigating my soup further, I'm pleased to discover chunks of pink ham. That is ham, right?

"And how was it?"

"It was fine. I was hoping for Kentucky Fried Chicken, but I think we had hot dogs or something. And we watched a film, which I probably found unrealistic."

"We didn't really have many sleepovers in my day," she says, "but that sounds about right."

"It was fine, initially. When it was time for bed, I was the last to brush my teeth. I was in the bathroom and opened my bag to get my PJs. I couldn't believe she had done this to me."

"Who, your mom?" Grandma is beginning to giggle, anticipating buffoonery.

"Yes, Mom. She'd packed my bloody Care Bear pajamas. I was mortified, Grandma. They were a matching top and bottom duet. There were images, action shots, of all the Care Bears on a lavender background."

"Those sound fine. You liked the Care Bears."

I cut a piece of the mushy banana for Grandma. It's starting to brown, but Grandma is unbothered by its indecent texture and accepts it on her side plate.

"I loved them; they were my runaway favourite PJs. But these were the goddamned Care Bears, Grandma, and I was sleeping in front of my hockey-obsessed buddies. The same guys who were steps down the hall, wearing very masculine Edmonton Oilers and Montreal Canadiens pajamas. I think one of them even had an Edmonton Oilers sleeping bag and pillowcase."

"Right, I understand," says Grandma, laughing more. "That could be a little embarrassing, I guess."

"Just wait," I say. "I emptied my bag, looking for any-thing else to wear. There was nothing. I had no options. I had to wear the damn bears. I brushed my teeth again and probably tried to comb my hair with wet fingers. I'm sure I was mentally dictating a vitriolic conniption toward Mom, which I would deliver the next day. When I finally left the bathroom, I was shirtless."

"Shirtless?"

"I'd put the bottoms on and realized, with just the silly trousers, it was tricky to discern the small shapes. From a few steps away they potentially could resemble small foot-ball players as much as magical, moral-expounding bears. So I left the top, which was much more explicitly beary, in the bag."

"Did your pals notice?" Grandma asks, with the faintest of grins. I sense she wants to laugh at me outright. We've been together long enough now that she's probably aban-doning the usual constraints of politeness.

"The first thing Felix asked when I got into the bedroom was, 'Hey, what's that?' 'What's what?' I answered. 'That,' he repeated, pointing toward my exposed tummy. It looked like plastic underwear was sticking up an inch or so above my waistband. 'What do you mean?' I asked. At this point, Grandma, I was honestly confused. I didn't know what he was asking about."

"What was it?"

"Felix reached his fingers out and tugged at the white material. 'This — what is this that you're wearing under your pants?' Finally I knew what he was talking about. 'Yeah, yeah,' I said, 'that's just my diaper.' I remember saying it as if it was the most natural and obvious thing in the world. My diaper!"

"Your what?"

"My diaper, Grandma, can you believe it? I was wearing a diaper and had no idea I was the only one. They were shocked. One of them asked why I was wearing a diaper."

"Oh, dear."

"I told them that of course I was, just like they were. It's the same, but the difference was you could see mine, because I wasn't wearing a shirt. I slapped my bare stomach and pulled up at the diaper. I was happy to elucidate why we could see mine and not theirs. I considered myself the brainy one of the group, so the role of explainer suited me. I believed that if they just lifted up their shirts, I could show them their own diapers. After all, we were all wearing them."

I pause for a spoonful of soup. Grandma nibbles at her banana.

"So John lifted up his shirt the way a gangster shows a gun. Felix did too. Neither was wearing a diaper. They told me they didn't wear diapers anymore. They hadn't for years. They told me they weren't babies."

"Poor Iain," says Grandma, chuckling.

"Here's what I learned at my first sleepover: I wasn't completely normal. Not everyone my age wore diapers. In fact, nobody did. And certainly not John or Felix. They had already stopped peeing in their sleep."

"You weren't a big bedwetter, though, were you?"

"No, it was maybe a biweekly occurrence. But it still happened. Since I was going to be in someone else's home, Mom thought it would be safe to wear one of my emergency diapers. They were called Big-Boy diapers or something because they looked more like underwear than your standard diaper. Mom assured me you couldn't see it under my pajamas and she packed it into my overnight bag. Of course, that logic only held when I was wearing both pants and shirt."

"Well, I can see why you'd remember that," she says.

"It probably helps explain why I appreciate solitude so much now. Whereas I think it's likely the opposite for most people — being alone is harder the older they get."

"You're probably right," she says.

"It does seem like there's less opportunity to be alone," I say. "How much time are people ever totally alone?" I push my bowl away with my left hand. "I'm not sure what I'm getting at."

"You're probably right," she says. And then, "Or maybe it's just harder to value it."

"I don't know, I'll go and sit in on certain lectures at the university sometimes. Sometimes I'll even write essays, but only theoretically. I don't actually write the papers but just construct them in my head as I walk home. I'll come up with counter-arguments and attempt to defend my imaginative case. It's strictly for me, for my own interest, so it's weirdly selfish. And in a week or so it's all forgotten, it's gone. Whereas when I talk about something I've been thinking about, like we are right now, it lingers. I'll remember this chat, so does that make it less selfish? Maybe that's why you shouldn't always be alone."

"Well, of course, there's that. That's just the tip of the iceberg, though, for the importance of others and closeness, right? There has to be a known end to the solitude. You have to know it's temporary for it to be enjoyed."

"Yeah, I guess so," I say. "I feel like our obsession with youth, or at least upholding the appearance of youth, is also related to our obsession with not wanting to be alone. Does that make any sense?"

"I think being alone is much easier when you don't feel alone," she says. "Feeling alone isn't the same as being alone."

I look down into my soup. I have some left but am feeling full. "You don't have to finish that, Grandma, if you don't want to."

"I love it," she says, tilting her bowl up to show me. It's already empty. "And not to worry, you've outgrown wetting the bed."

"Well, I guess so. For now, at least. I kinda wish I still had that silk scarf, though." And that Chopin tape. "What about some more soup then, Grandma? Would you like a top-up?"

"Sure," she says, "why not."

Her bowl looks pressure-washed clean. At the stove I turn away and sneeze twice before half-filling her bowl.

"Someone must be thinking about you," Grandma says as I set the bowl down in front of her.

"Pardon?"

"You sneezed," she says. "That's what we used to say after a sneeze, someone is thinking about you. That was a long time ago. But maybe it's still true. And you did it twice." She picks up her spoon. "So you never know."

I watch as Grandma peppers and then blows on her

second bowl of soup. I have my doubts, but she's right — you never do know.

2:31 p.m.

AFTER LUNCH I helped Grandma back to the comfortable chair so she could continue reading while I "cleaned up." I piled our dishes into the sink, adding to our medley from breakfast, and wiped the crumbs off the table with one hand into the other.

"Well, how's everything going?" I announce, carrying in a bubbly Aero bar I found in the cupboard. I open it and snap it into pieces on the wrapper. I lick the melted chocolate off my thumb and finger and set it on the coffee table. "Thought you might like a little dessert."

Grandma looks up from her book. It takes her a second to mentally escape its pages. She doesn't quite recognize me, and when she does, her reaction indicates she hasn't seen me in years. "Ahhhh... well, helllllo there." She's been holding her bookmark up on her shoulder and now puts it back to work, placing it between the pages. "I think you're getting taller. Is that possible?"

"I don't know about that."

"Yes, I really think so. And skinnier. You look leaner than you used to."

"Maybe, I'm not sure." I don't think my height or weight has changed in eight or so years. I take another step closer. "So, it's still raining pretty hard. Maybe harder."

"It does sound miserable out there."

We listen to the rain and I hold the wrapper up in front of her. "How 'bout a little chocolate?" I ask.

"Oh, sure," she says, taking two pieces of the candy. "What is it?"

"Just an Aero bar."

She eats her first piece. I watch her hardly shaky hand break off a small piece. She's very unfussy, I think. I don't think she's said no to anything I've offered. I suppose she would have declined chocolate-covered heart.

"I'm just loving this book," she says. "It's so interesting and different." She licks the melted chocolate off her fingers.

"What's it about?"

"It takes place in New Orleans. And I didn't know all that much about New Orleans and the criminal element there. It's all quite graphic and awful."

"Well, you could take a break from it and we could always watch a movie or something."

"Oh, okay. I don't get the chance to do that very often. I'd like that."

I'm not sure which movies I have lying around. I don't own many, but I always have a few out on loan from the library or video store. The only one I can find that I own is Trey Parker and Matt Stone's *BASEketball*. I'm not certain their target audience is Grandma.

I find a stack of rentals. There are two possibilities. Woody Allen's *Broadway Danny Rose* and an animated film, *Coraline*. I'm sure Grandma hasn't seen either, so I flip a coin in my head.

Coraline wins.

My impromptu movie plan affords me the chance to

make a batch of popcorn. Like the brewed coffee, it's without a shadow of doubt one of my best creations. I've invented this spice mixture that puts the traditional salt and butter to absolute shame. I can't reveal everything I put into this dry rub, but included are paprika, cumin, and cayenne.

I leave Grandma to contemplate the previews while I pop our corn. It fills my apartment with a philharmonic pinging as the hard yellow kernels erupt into white puffy clouds. I pour them into two wooden bowls and toss them liberally with my spice mix.

For one noisy moment, I am great, and so is this trip.

"It smells so good," she says as I walk in. It looks like Grandma may have fallen asleep while waiting. The DVD menu is up on the screen, and the film's musical score is playing in a fifteen-second loop.

I hand her a bowl and a napkin. "Are you ready to start?" I say.

"Yes," she says.

"Okay, sorry, just let me run to the bathroom first."

Half an hour later I've made another trip to the bathroom, have put on and taken off my sweater, have polished off my bowl, and am using my tongue to pick at the kernel skins wedged between my teeth. I'm enjoying the film, but I'm concerned Grandma can't hear it. I also don't want to turn it up too loud and make her think *I think* she's deaf and thus old. So I'm trying to raise the volume subtly. This is tricky because every time I turn it up a notch I have to walk to the TV, and with each increment a graphic appears on the screen showing the new, higher volume. It's all profoundly unsubtle.

"Are you sure you can hear it, Grandma?" I ask for the fourth or fifth time.

"Oh, yes, dear, of course."

I'm not so sure. It's pretty damn loud, though. So I leave it. On my way back to my seat I notice Grandma's complexion looking unmistakably flushed. She looks sweaty and flustered. I ask her if everything's all right. What would make her suddenly hot and bothered? An age thing? I hope it's not serious. What if it's her thyroid?

"I'm fine, dear, maybe a little warm."

"Warm?"

"Yes, I think perhaps from that popcorn. It's good, but was it a spicy flavour?"

Fuck! I spiced both bowls evenly. And I was heavy-handed. Each kernel was wearing a heavy parka of cayenne. Maybe this is serious. Maybe this kind of thing can really do her some damage.

"Do you feel light-headed or faint, Grandma?" Should I get her to lie down? Maybe she needs to stand up. I'm above her now, fanning her with the open DVD case.

She looks over at me, raising that one eyebrow again. "Oh, heavens, no. I'm fine. I'd love a glass of water but that's it." She waves me away and coughs savagely.

I run back into the kitchen. I'm sweating now, too. I'm finding it hard to steady my hand as I hold a finger under the running water, waiting for it to cool.

THE PHONE CALL that disrupted the last scene of the movie was worth it. I left Grandma to watch (or sleep) and jogged into the kitchen to answer it. It was the fellow from the water tank place. He's coming tomorrow. We'll have hot water starting then. Finally, some good news. The credits are scrolling upward when I return.

I don't think she enjoyed the film. I don't think she hated it. I don't think she heard very much of it. She may have been asleep for a large chunk.

Her reaction: "That was just so different." She's been saying this a lot. She's said it about food and books we've talked about and now an animated movie. *It's just so different*—a purposefully neutral comment delivered with a positive inflection.

It's dark when I switch off the television. I hadn't detected it was the TV lighting the room. I'm famished. "I don't think you should have to cook again," Grandma says when I mention supper.

I replay my day of "cooking" in my head: toasted some frozen bread, opened some cheese, warmed up some canned soup in a pot, opened a chocolate bar, made some borderline–catastrophically infused popcorn.

"You know, I don't mind *actually* cooking some supper."

"Well, I think we should go out, dear. My treat. This week is a celebration, after all."

"No, no way, Grandma. Not a chance. I'm supposed to be treating you. This is a trip for you!"

"Why don't you pick where we go, then. That's fair."

"Hardly." But there's no use arguing. Trust me. Grandma's made up her mind. That eyebrow of hers is twitching wildly.

8:49 p.m.

THE ONLY PARKING spot I can find near the restaurant is a ridiculously tight fit. It's directly in front of a generic sports bar with groups of baseball-hatted lads loitering in front. A crowd never makes parking any easier. I choose to go for it because it's late, I'm hungry, and we've driven around in a circle twice now looking for something better. Grandma is humming. She wonders if the bar is a new one. "It looks new to me," she says.

"I'm not sure, Grandma," I say, looking over my left shoulder, then my right, as we inch backward. "I think it's been here for a while." It's a very old bar, but I don't have the heart to say anything.

I have to verbally wrangle a smoker outside the pub to stand behind my car and direct me as I parallel into place. It's an embarrassing question made worse when he asks me to repeat my request twice. "I . . . need your help guiding me into the space," I say again. He's finding the situation more comical than embarrassing. Grandma is offering her sincere encouragement.

"It's such a tricky spot, you're doing great," she's saying.

My wheels — or the steering column, or whatever it is — are squeaking piercingly. I'm moving very slowly. The smoker is unimpressed. "Your left tire is right up on the friggin' curb, man," I hear through my open window.

"Right," I say. "Thanks."

"This might be the best parking job I've ever seen," Grandma adds.

"Right," I say. "Thanks."

Grandma can't hear him. He can't hear Grandma. There is a mere five or six feet separating them. Perspective is everything.

Out on the sidewalk I take a moment and admire my handiwork while I wait for Grandma to make her way around the car. We both thank the smoker for his friggin' help.

The rain has let up but is still keeping non-smokers indoors. Kingston is not a big city like Toronto or Montreal, where regardless of weather, the streets are continually busy. The earlier rain has chased everyone away, or inside. On these nights Kingston feels hollow, like the set of a film that's done shooting for the day.

It's a short walk, a couple of blocks to the restaurant. We stroll slowly. No cars pass us. I ask Grandma if she wants me to carry her purse. She smiles but says no, almost defensively, slinging the strap up higher on her shoulder.

"AND THE ONLY thing we had was an icebox."

"Sorry, Grandma?"

"An icebox. That was all."

"You mean in your house?"

"Yup, that was it."

"How did that work?"

The restaurant feels empty enough to make me feel guilty for taking us here. I know it's raining, but people still have to eat, right? Before the parking circus, we had driven farther out of the city, toward the suburbs, but the restaurant I had in mind there was already closed. So we got back in my car and returned downtown.

The young hostess seemed surprised we wanted a table. She was standing at her post, wiping down the laminated floor plan in front of her. She was using a white paper towel, which was stained with blue marker. She regarded me incriminatingly, leading the way without a word. Grandma doesn't appear concerned.

"It was just what it sounds like. A wooden box, and we would put a large chunk of ice in the back."

"To keep your food from spoiling?"

"Yup, obviously we didn't have a fridge or freezer in those days, just the icebox."

"Imagine trying to live without a fridge or freezer now. Or imagine trying to run this restaurant with a bloody icebox!"

After scanning the large room I realize only one other table is occupied. It's a large group. There are a few bottles of wine on the tables, which have been pushed together. By the way they sit, and their messy table full of crumpled napkins, I assume they're on the back nine of their meal. Probably graduate students on one of their weekly celebrations. In grad school, unlike life, it's always someone's birthday. The hostess drops off some water and our menus, and tells us our server will be by shortly.

"Nothing was ever wasted. I can't remember ever throwing anything away because it had spoiled." A wooden chair is tipped over at the table of students. "Never, not once." No one is in the chair, but the empty thud and the resulting laughter cause Grandma to look over.

I'm categorically leery of refrigerated leftovers older than forty-eight hours. That's typically my cutoff. I find them intimidating. Conversely, this morning I watched in sheer disgust as Grandma plunged her face into a Tupperware of week-old spaghetti sauce for a whiff. Later she dipped a finger into some antediluvian ranch salad dressing. Food age is irrelevant to her. She judges strictly with her senses.

When it comes to aging food, I avoid reason and rely on imagination. Once I ate a crumb of green mould the size of a sunflower seed that was growing on a piece of mildly stale bread. I was living in Toronto at the time and was alone when it happened. I'd been famished and had eaten half a slice before doing my standard physical examination of the loaf to ensure no signs of discolouration. I saw the mould, post-swallow, on the rest of the loaf that I had put down on the counter. I remember immediately calling my Aunt Charlotte, an emergency physician.

"What should I do now?" I asked. "Just wait out the storm, or toss a finger down my throat?"

"What? No, no, you're fine."

"Fine? Didn't you hear what I said?"

"I think I did."

"I ate mould."

She laughed at me — *directly at me* — and eventually talked me off the ledge. I woke up once or twice in the night with belly cramps.

"You know, I could eat a steak tonight," Grandma says. I hadn't noticed her pick up her menu. She's not looking at it, just holding it.

"Yeah, that does sound pretty good."

I'm not sure if it's because we're here so late, or if this is just a restaurant that purposefully keeps its lighting dim.

It's dark. We have two tea lights on our table. They aren't lit. It's dark enough that even the light provided by two small candles would help. I don't mind it, but it can't be easy for Grandma's eyes.

"Can you see steak anywhere on the menu?" Grandma is holding her menu with both hands. She's still not looking at it.

"There's a steak sandwich here," I point out, "with onion rings and horseradish mayo."

"That's what I'm getting," she says, closing her menu determinedly. "I don't even have to look at anything else."

"And it comes with blackened potato salad."

"With what?"

"Oh, blackened potato salad."

"Sorry, dear, I didn't hear that..." She leans closer.

"It's POTATO SALAD...BLACKENED..."

"Potato...sala'blacken...I've never had that."

"Yeah, well, it's very good."

"It sounds pretty good."

We order our sandwiches. I ask for well done. Grandma does the same, an unexpected surprise. I hate when I'm with people (usually my dad) who tell me how I'm ruining my meat by asking for well done. A steak has to be rare, they say. I say meat should be cooked through. How does the presence of blood on your plate increase the level of enjoyment? I feel like me, Stonewall Jackson, and now Grandma are the only people in history who appreciate grey, dry steak.

I also ask for a half-litre of house red, first confirming Grandma will share. "Oh, why not," she says. "I'm not driving."

When the wine arrives, our indifferent server pours Grandma's first. Isn't she curious why I'm here with an old lady? Doesn't she want to ask why Grandma is up so late? We "cheers" and touch glasses. I sip mine. Grandma sniffs hers. The server's already gone.

"I can still remember when slacks came into style for women. Before, it was all dresses and skirts." I didn't see this topic coming. Our server is wearing a pair of blue pants that somehow look tighter than her skin. "Imagine that, only wearing dresses every day."

"No, I can't."

"What I think I'll always remember is my very first pair of slacks. My mom bought them for me. I loved them. They were called whoopie pants."

I rise in my chair, shifting my weight to the opposite buttock. "Whoopie pants, okay."

"Yes, they were great. I can still remember them vividly. You see, I was just lucky, no one else I knew had whoopies. I was the only one."

"I'd like to see a pair of these whoopie pants, Grandma. I can't picture them." I look up toward the ceiling as if a replica of the pants has been stencilled there. Instead, in the dim light I can make out what appears to be a large yellow stain in the shape of a chubby wiener dog.

Grandma takes a few minutes to explain the nuts and bolts, the structural makeup of the pants. I'm finding it difficult to imagine the unusual garment. I've cobbled together a murky image. I'm seeing a pair of trousers that are essentially the opposite of bell-bottoms; tight near the bottom and loose from the knees up, almost MC Hammer–ish or Elizabethan.

"What are the women your age wearing, dear? I try, but it's hard for me to keep up."

I sip my wine, more generously this time, and cross my legs. "Styles seem to come and go so quickly, don't they?" I say expertly. I realize I don't have any authority when it comes to fashion, especially women's fashion. I still wear the grey toque I wore in middle school, and trousers cut into shorts with white tube socks in the summer. "I guess I usually just try to predict to myself which trends will become reviled the quickest."

"That will what?" Grandma leans in again over the table.

"Like, I mean, which styles will be out of fashion the soonest."

"Oh," she says.

"For example, Grandma, have you noticed those gladiator-style sandals that a lot of women are wearing these days?" Our server is currently sporting a pair. Grandma doesn't say anything but looks at me and smiles. "Well, there are several different styles of these sandals but I find them all unbecoming. I don't know why. Too many straps and buckles and leather. Especially because flats, like the ballet slipper style" — which our hostess is wearing — "are still popular and, I think, much more flattering." I look up from my plate to see Grandma smoothing out her napkin over her legs, which I've noticed she likes to do. Over and over. I've lost her. "Anyway, getting back to the whoopies, I would love to see them."

"Yes, the whoopie pants. I wonder if anyone still has a pair locked away in some closet. Iain, dear, I never knew you had such an interest in women's fashion. It's great," she says, reaching across the table, putting her hand on mine. It's the first time she's done something like this. "I've known you all these years and there's still so much I'm learning about you."

WE'RE ONLY BITES — me many and Grandma two — into our meal when I detect that her sandwich is missing the promised horseradish mayo. She doesn't seem bothered by the miscue. But I am. It's a worthy addition.

"Here, Grandma, take some of this sauce, it's pretty good."

"No, no, that's yours. I'm fine, really."

I beckon the sandalled waitress over with a hand wave. "Um, sorry, but you guys forget the horseradish sauce for her steak." I also want to suggest that covering her diaphoretic feet while she's serving food isn't a dreadful idea.

"Okay." She offers her watch a tiny glance, surely for our benefit — a quick visual memo of how late it is. "I'll be right back."

I don't know why, but before she walks away I blurt that Grandma is ninety-two. The server freezes, takes a step back, looks over Grandma, and declares, "Amazing." Her delivery is too actressy, and the word is laced with a carsalesman panache. I immediately regret saying anything.

For a while we refocus on our fare. We're hungry. We eat and drink. And then Grandma sets her cutlery down on the sides of her plate like the oars of a boat. She carefully wipes both sides of her mouth and swallows before speaking. "It was my dad who came out to Canada first, you know, before the rest of the family."

"No, I didn't know that." I set my own fork down.

"Oh, sure. I suppose the plan was to get settled with a job and such. And then we would come after. I never asked him why Canada or even why they decided we should leave Scotland."

"They must have had a reason."

"He didn't have much training for work. He'd been a baker in the Old Country. But when he got to Canada, the only work he could get was as a labourer. He looked after horses, because his father had had a horse-and-cart business back in Scotland. They transported fish to London. Anyway, it wasn't long then, before any of the rest of us came over, that the war broke out in Europe and he signed up with the Canadian army."

"First World War?"

"Yup. He fought overseas. And luckily, he survived. We all moved out to the Prairies after the war. He started working as a custodian in a school. We really got on well. I got along best with my dad, I think. He'd tease me all the time. Once, I fell asleep after dinner and he took some ash from the fireplace and smudged a dark mustache above my lip. He'd also do things like, if we were all sitting at the table for tea, he'd just take his spoon out of his hot tea after stirring it and without saying anything place it down on my hand." Grandma puts her index finger onto the back of my hand in place of a hot spoon. "Just like that. I'd always make a big fuss, like I was completely shocked, like it really burned. But I always knew it was coming. That was the whole thing."

Grandma starts to cough as if the memory has dislodged a small piece of food in the back of her throat. She holds her hand up to say she's okay, but takes a sip of her water, then her wine. Her face is still red from coughing when she continues.

"He fought at Vimy. But he couldn't talk about it."

"Ever?"

"No, never. And after the war he always got tight on Christmas Day and Remembrance Day. Other than that he never drank."

"Really?"

"Yup. Maybe he told my mother everything that happened, I don't know, but not us kids. I just know the way he was and his personality and I know it would have been very hard on him, seeing all the things he saw. When I got older and read about what happened at Vimy and in the trenches and what he would have seen..."

She pauses. It's difficult to tell if she's going to cough again. Her eyes are full of life and expression and are going on without her, trying to finish her story non-verbally. I have to look away.

I wonder how I would do in war. How I would cope with life in a foxhole or trench? I grew up on a small farm, played sports, studied at university, and then started working. The idea of being engaged in active combat, sleeping in mud with fleas and rats, eating limited rations, and seeing my friends injured and killed seems almost beyond comprehension to me.

"Anyway, he stopped going to church after the war, too. He never went again."

"I'm sure it changed him in a lot of ways."

"I think so. They didn't know about post-traumatic stress disorder back then." Grandma looks down at her plate. She picks up her cutlery and cuts a piece of dry steak and slides an onion ring with her knife onto the fork. "And when he died, I got a leather baby boot without the laces . . . oh, I'm sorry to go on like this, you probably want to eat."

"No, this is interesting."

"Well, it was actually my own baby boot. I never knew it at the time, but he'd taken it with him to France. He'd used it as a holder for his coins."

She puts the forkful of food into her mouth and starts chewing. "I can't imagine how good it would have been for his money. It was such a little boot . . . it really was tiny."

AFTER OUR SANDWICHES and potato salad, Grandma wonders if I want dessert. I tell her I'm fine. I'm full. I'm content just to finish off the wine. She says the same to our server, who drops off our cheque with two plastic-wrapped clear mints. Again Grandma asks me to fill in the Visa slip with an appropriate tip, and then she signs it.

On our walk back to the car, Grandma takes my arm.

"It's on nights like this my nose starts up like a tap. Whenever there's a bit of a chill in the air."

I sniff. "Actually, yeah, me too," I say.

It's my right forearm she holds, looping her hand around my elbow. She typically likes to walk on her own strength, so I'm not sure if it's because she's tired, or is feeling the wine, or just because.

"Don't you find it funny when people always say, 'Don't go to sleep angry'?" Grandma says suddenly.

"Yeah, I guess," I say. "You hear that a lot. It's become a bit of a relationship cliché, hasn't it?"

We walk slowly and carefully, avoiding the thin puddles.

"It is, it's a cliché, just something that people say because it sounds right. I can tell you now, in any long, meaningful relationship you're going to go to bed some nights angry and frustrated and upset."

"You're probably right, seems more realistic."

"Of course. No one can upset you or irritate you more than the one you're married to. These things aren't easy. It's more important not to take the other person for granted the rest of the time, when you're not angry."

We stop to catch our breath and both use a Kleenex on our runny noses.

"If you ever want to really know how you feel about someone ..." she says.

"Yeah ..."

"Look at them when they're asleep," she says, and starts walking again. I follow.

"Really?"

"Yup. If you're ever married some day and you're mad at your wife, wait for a while, until she's definitely fallen asleep. Give it a bit of time. Then roll over and just have a look at her. Then you'll know how you feel. That's the important part, the looking."

"Just look?"

"Everyone always talks about communicating and talking through an argument, which I suppose is important. But I would say, try to be quiet." Grandma looks up with grinning eyes. "But they have to be asleep for it to work."

IT'S A SHORT drive back to my place. I leave the radio off. I don't play any tapes. All we hear is the engine and tires on the road. Grandma gazes out her window the whole way, at the lake and the trees. I pull into my driveway. Grandma gets out first and walks around the front of the car. The rain has now completely stopped, not even a drizzle, but the air still feels heavy and damp, like a giant bedsheet taken out of the dryer too soon.

"I was hoping the stars would be brighter, now that the rain has stopped," says Grandma. "But you can't really see them."

"I guess it's still cloudy up there."

"It's always nice to be able to see them. It's a perk of being out this late."

"True."

"Maybe if we look up long enough they'll start to come out. Maybe our eyes just need to adjust."

I swing my door closed and walk around my side to the front of the car. It's actually not *that* late. It feels later than it is. Especially on my street. It's a street full of families and young couples. The other homes are notable only for their darkness.

"It's so nice here. And quiet," says Grandma.

"Yes, it is."

"And the smell," she says. "It smells amazing tonight after that rain."

"It does, doesn't it? *Petrichor*, that's the word."

Grandma doesn't respond. We take a moment to smell. I smell the air. Grandma does the same. How many more breaths has she inhaled and exhaled than I have? Obviously thousands, hundreds of thousands. Maybe millions? We're inhaling and exhaling deep breaths as if small breaths are corrupting for the lungs.

"It reminds me of a lake," I say. "Or any large body of water."

"Yes, and I was thinking of a bonfire for some reason." She inhales again. "Yes, definitely a bonfire. Maybe someone isn't asleep. Maybe someone has a fire going. I like that idea."

I waft the air à la scientist-over-beaker. "Agreed," I say. "I'm getting fire now, too."

I haven't just stood outside my place at night like this for a long time. Maybe never. It's mighty pleasant. I look back and see Grandma's left her door ajar. It hangs open like the mouth of someone who's surprised. When I get over to close it for her, I decide it looks less surprised and more like it's holding a wide yawn.

12:44 a.m.

"GRANDMA, IS EVERYTHING all right?"

"Yes, dear, I'm fine."

"Are you sure? I thought you'd gone to bed."

"Yes, I had," she says. "I thought you had, too."

We both had. We'd gone inside, each drinking a coffee mug of water, and said we were tired. I gave her a pat on the back and we went to our rooms.

"Yeah, I had. But I'm not sure if all that food is sitting right with me. I have some gurglies or something."

Grandma brushes a thin tuft of bang off her forehead. I'm not used to seeing her like this: in her nightgown, barefoot, with her hair unbrushed. The nails on her toes are gnarled and thick. I can't decide if she looks older or younger.

"What's the problem?" she asks.

I think maybe she looks older. "Oh, nothing, I have heartburn or something. I think I have some TUMS in the bathroom."

"Oh, that's a shame. Is it very bad?"

"My tummy? It's not great, but not lethal. How's yours?" I'm anticipating a similar complaint from Grandma. We ate identical meals and drank identical drinks.

"Oh, it's fine. I just loved that potato sala'blacken," she says.

"Then why are you up?"

"I was just going to check the hockey score. We forgot to do that when we got home."

"Oh, you mean on the TV?"

"Yes, exactly."

I cross my arms over my stomach. "Well, do you know how to turn it on or do you want me to do that?"

"No, no, you go get your medicine and get better. I can figure it out." She's already three steps down the hall and talking over her left shoulder. "Feel better, dear."

After my tummy pills and another mug of water, I burp three times back to back to back and feel remarkably better. I walk by the living room a new man. My small TV is an old one, and has no remote. Grandma is bent over in front, working the buttons with one hand. She's found the sports channel and is lowering the volume now. Her back is arched.

"So how'd the Senators do, Grandma?" I call.

She turns her head carefully, still locked in her quasi-hunch. She's not pushing the buttons anymore but is holding the front of the TV. She's using it as a brace. Her smile blooms across her face.

"I had a feeling we'd do it," she says, pumping a fist over her head. "The boys won!"

WEDNESDAY

7:56 a.m.

MY FIRST CONSCIOUS thought this morning is a delightful one: I can't hear rain. Almost as nice, no beeping alarm. I've beat it to the punch. I'm awake first. My room is quiet. I'm not exhausted. I'm in the vicinity of well-rested. Not much tossing and turning. No Lynchian nightmares. No head-ache, and my stomach feels right again. The knots from last night have been unlaced.

I wonder how Grandma's doing?

We've made it through two days, and presumably two nights, without any mishaps or injury or irritation. That's something. It's all been startlingly pleasant.

My calm reverie is disrupted when I hear something metallic hit something metallic. A piece of cutlery dropped into an empty sink? Grandma must be awake. She's up already? I roll out of bed, grab my housecoat, and step into my slippers.

"Grandma," I say, shuffling into the kitchen, tying my robe at the waist, "good morn. You beat me up. Well, I mean, you didn't physically harm me, but . . . you're up!"

I'm getting used to seeing her first thing. It's less awk-ward. For both of us. This morning her grin, white hair, rounded shoulders, and twinkling eyes feel almost as habitual as the smell of coffee.

"Yes, dear, I woke up early to take my pill and just decided to stay up. I've been reading. It's so nice and quiet."

I take a step closer. She's sitting at the puny table. There's something in her voice that sounds coarser. It looks like she's coloured her left nostril with a red crayon. "Are you feeling okay?"

"Yes, sure, I'm fine. I had another great sleep. You know me."

"'Cause you sound a little hoarse, or something. Or stuffed up."

"Oh, yes, well, not to worry. I'm fine." She looks down at her lap and sniffs. "I've caught something. But it's just a small cold in my nose, nothing serious."

I've never considered a flu or cold "small" before. Anytime I'm sick, or even mildly ill, I revert to my four-year-old self. I'm unamused and sulk around feeling sorry for myself, questioning my life choices, yearning for simultaneous peace, quiet, *and* constant twenty-four-hour care.

Grandma's voice sounds worse than a "small cold." I don't press her. I don't want her thinking I'm worried about it. "Okay, well, how do you feel? Do you want to go back to bed or anything? I could give you some extra blankets."

Offering blankets: isn't that what one does?

"No, no, of course not. I'm up. I'm fine." Her body calls her a liar as she sneezes into the crook of her arm. She'd been trying to stifle the urge. Then she lifts her head up for a second, shuts her eyes, and sneezes again. The double sneeze accentuates the glaze in her eyes. Her face is drawn.

It looks longer and thinner than it did yesterday. Her hair is combed, but not quite as meticulously as yesterday or the day before. It's flatter.

"Well, let me at least get you something warm to drink. Tea or coffee?"

"Whatever's easier, dear."

"Both are extremely easy."

"Some tea would be lovely. Thank you," she says, clearing her throat.

I set the kettle to boil and myself to brood. I'm mentally whistling along with the kettle, ready to be taken off my own burning element of worry and disappointment. Now she's sick!? Really? I'll clearly have to put her to bed. She'll spend all today and tomorrow sleeping. Then it'll be time to take her home.

I can easily predict the culmination to our glorious holiday. I'll start to feel my throat tighten up. I'll sneeze a few times as I drive her home. On my way back to Kingston it'll settle in on me earnestly. I'm going to catch this cold. I'm not *actually* worried about that, though. Honestly. I don't care if I get it. Seriously. I can cope with a stupid cold. I'm younger. My main concern is for Grandma and her well-being.

No. I *am* worried about getting it. I don't want the cold. Completely Fucking Pathetic. CFP, that should be my nickname from now on. I should sign emails *Yours,* CFP.

"Here you go, Grandma," I say, setting her tea down in front of her with my arm fully extended. I'm maintaining a germ-free buffer zone between us. "Now what about something to eat?"

"You know, dear, I'm really not all that hungry this morning. I'm not sure I could eat anything. Just the tea, I think. But you should have something."

"No, no, I don't have to eat anything either. I'm okay with just a cup of coffee." Not true at all.

"That's ridiculous. It won't bother me to watch you eat. My stomach isn't upset."

I don't put up much of a fight. In fact, I relent aggressively, not just toasting an English muffin but filling the kitchen with the smells of bacon, eggs, beans, fried potatoes, tomatoes, and toast.

I gorge and convince Grandma to take some toast and potato. And then some egg, too. And a piece of bacon. "It just smelled so good," she says. "And I guess I still have my appetite."

After using her piece of toast as an edible J Cloth to wipe her plate clean, Grandma finally asks me what she's been wanting to ask all morning (and potentially all night). "Do you have Kleenex, dear?"

"Oh, I'm sorry, Grandma. Yes, of course, my God, I should have thought of that," I say, jumping up out of my chair.

"That's fine. I usually have some on me."

I run back to my room. I look everywhere. I throw my pillows onto the floor and knock a stack of books off my desk. I ransack the bathroom. I can't find Kleenex anywhere. Plan B (which really should have been more like plan Q): I wrap a generous bundle of toilet paper around my hand and rip it from its roll. I sheepishly lay it on the table in front of Grandma.

"Very sorry, Grandma. I actually don't have any real Kleenex. But I have lots of toilet paper, so feel free to go to town." Go to town? On the toilet paper? I want to grab the words out of the air as I'm saying them, wrap them in the toilet paper, and flush them away.

"Oh, this will do fine." She picks it up immediately and does what she's been wanting to do all morning — give her nose a hearty blow.

I decide, under the shameless protection of the blowing-her-nose din, that now's the time to mention my morning plans. "I hope you don't mind, but we have to wait for these water guys to get here." I say it quickly to finish at the same time as her blowing.

"Who are the water guys?" wonders Grandma as she takes the remainder of the toilet paper and slides it up under her shirt sleeve. I can still see it, hanging from her forearm like a white tail.

"I mean the guys who are going to fix the hot water tank."

"Oh, okay. Yes, that's fine. The hot water tank is broken?"

For the first time I realize Grandma hasn't mentioned the lack of hot water. She's been here for two nights. She hasn't said a word about it. How could that be? Is this because she hasn't required any hot water? Or because she didn't want to say anything because she didn't want me to feel bad?

"Yeah, sorry, I thought I told you, Grandma." Maybe I did tell her? It's possible she just forgot. "They said they'd be here sometime this morning. They didn't have an exact time."

"Fine, dear. That's just fine."

"Are you sure you don't want to go back to bed? We have to stick around anyway."

"No, I'm fine."

"Well, then, what do you feel like doing? We can't really go anywhere until they get here." We've become like two children sitting in a basement on a Saturday afternoon with nowhere to go. And nothing to do.

"Whatever you think. But first, could you do me a favour?"

"Sure, anything."

I'm assuming she's going to ask me to pop out and obtain some cold medication. Maybe some chicken soup and Kleenex. "Would you mind just opening the cupboard there, under the sink?"

"Oh, okay. Sure." I stand and do as requested. I watch Grandma ball up her used squares of toilet paper. She steadies her hand and lets the paper fly like a mini mucus basketball. Her form is pristine. It lands in the rubbish bin square in the middle. *Swish.* She smiles.

I'm wide-eyed in approval and surprised at her shot. "Hey, how would you like to see my desk?" This is a release of uncensored verbal cogitation. I'm impressed by her trashbasket shot, but instead of saying so have brought up my desk. I don't know why.

Maybe it's because subconsciously I'm aware they have something in common, Grandma and my desk. Both are sturdy and have lived in several different places, in different homes. And both are very old. I would say both are reliable. I've been getting to know each one better, the older they get.

Without asking me to repeat the question or taking a moment to consider this new topic, she answers, "Yes, I'd love to see it. I know how much you like your desk."

Without another word, I lead her to my room. There isn't much to see. I have a reading chair, a record player, some bookcases. I have a bed without a frame. It sits on the floor. I hastily make my bed, which I'd neglected to do, as Grandma peers around.

"This is a cozy room. It's so nice that you have some plants." She's talking about my aloe vera plant sitting on the window ledge. It's an insignificant plant, my only one, and could probably fit in a medium-sized coffee cup. But by definition it is a plant. It is green. And both Grandma and I appreciate greenery.

"Yeah, I like having something alive in here to keep me company. But the best part, Grandma, take at look at this." I take her by the arm over to my desk. I pull out the chair and take the hoodie off the back.

"Oh, my. Wow. Look at this," she says, seating herself.

My desk is the best desk in the world. It's solid oak. It's sturdy. And it's ancient. There are scratches on it, not all over it, and the drawers are a bit sticky. It really is perfect. Grandma delicately runs her hand over the top. Like her, it has a past that reveals itself every time I find another scratch or set of initials scraped onto its surface.

"I just love it," she says. "It's exactly what I pictured."

I consider it priceless, but I actually got my desk for free. When I first moved to Kingston, I was in need of a desk. Any desk. I'd been writing on the tiny space atop a broken sewing machine from the 1970s. There was no room for any papers, so I had to scatter any notes over the floor and my neighbouring bed. I would have settled for any salvageable horizontal working surface.

I'd been browsing online, but nothing in my price range was significantly better than the blasted sewing machine. One morning I happened to take a stroll down a neighbouring street. It was early. I came across my desk sitting at the end of a driveway. It wasn't my desk yet but was about to be. It had a handwritten note Scotch-taped to the front: "*FREE*." The drawers were all out and sitting on top as if proving it had nothing to hide.

"I guess it was meant to be. That's so lucky," she says, swivelling around to face me again.

"Do you think you're lucky?" I ask.

"Absolutely. I am. I've always been lucky."

"Really? You mean, when you look back at things that have happened to you?"

"I mean now. I think feeling lucky is really only important, really only helpful, in the present. It seems tempting to wait for perspective, perspective gained by time. But it becomes irrelevant in the past. Luck doesn't really mean the same thing if it's only understood through memory, is what I'm trying to say."

She stands again and pushes the chair back under the desk. She walks over to my bookcase. "You sure like books, don't you."

"I like to read . . ."

She pulls the odd one out, reading the spine before sliding it back in. "I should borrow a couple from you. You know, new ones. It's hard for me to know what new books to pick."

"Did your parents read much when you were young?"

"I don't think so, not much. The papers maybe, but not books so much."

She walks over to my hi-fi sitting on its stand by the wall. "Is that an old record player?" she asks.

"Yeah, it is."

"We used to have a gramophone that was built into a large armoire. We really only had Scottish music, though."

"I have some records in my closet."

"Really? I'd love to see some. Would you mind?"

"No, not at all."

I scurry into my closet and retrieve two of my milk crates of albums. I lug one and drag the other over to Grandma. I tell her to sit in the comfy chair beside the bookcase. She does and folds her hands together on her lap. I sit down on the floor. "I think there'll be a few in here you'll remember."

I start flipping through the collection. When I come across those I think she'll remember, I pass them to her. Some sleeves are quite damaged and ripped, and I have to be careful to ensure a delicate hand-off: quarterback to running back without fumble.

"You probably used to listen to this," I say.

She receives each and examines it closely. After we've isolated five or six, I suggest maybe we put one on. "What do you think, Grandma? Do you want to listen to some of these while we wait?"

"I'd love that. Let's start with this one," she says. She hands me the Ink Spots.

"Grandma," I say, nodding, "great choice."

I put it on. The speakers spit and crackle and then go quiet before the music starts. We listen to the first two tracks entirely without speaking. Neither of us makes any noise, no coughing or sniffing. We're like two audio sponges, soaking up the resonance equally. I'm lying on the floor, my hands under my head. Grandma puts her feet up on the stool and leans back.

She's listening with strict attention. She even closes her eyes. I furtively watch as her face goes from resolute pleasure to careful regard. She's thinking about something and wants to talk. She shifts forward.

"I do love the old records," she says, opening her eyes. "It's a different sound."

"It's nice, isn't it?"

"We've always listened to music in our family, haven't we."

"Yeah, we always did growing up."

"My dad loved music. And, like your grandpa, he loved to dance."

"Was he good?"

"My dad was a wonderful dancer. That's how I learned. He taught me. But it wasn't like you see in the movies, when a child is learning to dance and they stand on the feet of their much older partner. No, it was real dancing we did." She pauses. "At least it seemed like it to me. I just know I didn't do anything silly like stand on his feet."

"What kind of music did you listen to then?"

"Mostly whatever was on the radio. We always had the radio on after supper . . ." She turns away and brings a hand up to her mouth.

"What is it?"

"Oh, nothing. Sorry, just thinking about all these old stories. I haven't thought about these things in such a long time." She faces me again. "You know, my dad was never a letter writer. But when he was back fighting in France, not long after I was born, he wrote a letter home to Scotland. It was for me. I still remember how it started: 'Dear Sweetheart.' I kept it for a long time, but I'm not sure what happened to it. I've kept a lot of things over the years, but I've probably lost just as many."

"Your memory is excellent. That's what I have to worry about. I can't remember very much from my childhood and it wasn't all that long ago."

"Oh, I don't know about that. You told me some stories yesterday."

"I guess." Although I'd be just as happy to forget about that diaper episode.

"Anyway, my sisters were often around, and my brother Pat loved music, too."

"I'm not sure I know much about Pat."

"Pat and I got along very well. I can remember him rubbing my back if I couldn't sleep. We were all different, but a close family. And because there was such an age difference between myself and the older siblings, they were almost like parents."

"What happened to Pat?"

"He died young. He had a heart attack shovelling snow. We were in Canada when it happened, and I can remember my mom getting the phone call."

"What about your sisters, what happened to them?"

"Which ones?"

"How many did you have again?" I think there were a lot of them.

"Sisters?"

"Well, brothers *and* sisters. There were quite a few of you, right?"

Grandma knows everything about my tiny family. I have only two siblings and no cousins. I know very little about hers. I know more today than I did three days ago. Still, I don't even know exactly how many siblings she had. I do know she's the only one left.

"There were seven of us. Well, really there were eight. Chinsy was the oldest. Her real name was Johanne, but we only ever called her Chinsy. Then Pat, whose real name was Peter. Lottie was next. She was Charlotte, but we called her Lottie."

"Huh, Lottie from Charlotte. I like that."

Grandma starts laughing and closes her eyes. "It's actually quite ridiculous when I think about it now. We had nicknames for everyone."

"I like it."

"I suppose if you use a nickname to someone's face it means you like them."

"True."

"Anyway, after Lottie was Jean. Her actual name was Jane. She was a real ham, a joker. She loved to tease and laugh. Next was Della. Her full name was Donnella. Okay, so after those five there was a fourteen-year gap before the next baby. And that was me. And then the youngest, Donald. Donald was four years younger than me. My only younger sibling, my baby brother. That's seven, right?"

"Yup."

"The eighth wasn't my parents' baby. But they raised him. That was Dean. He was just a baby when he came to live with us."

"Yeah, I remember hearing that name, Dean. But I can't remember who he was."

"He also died quite young, during surgery."

The record stops abruptly. I hear the needle lift and return to its resting position. "Should we listen to another one?" asks Grandma, interrupting herself.

"Yeah, sure. Which one?"

"You pick this time." I roll over onto my stomach and flip through a few. "How about this one?" I ask, holding up an Artie Shaw album.

"Yeah," she says.

"Or maybe..." I flip through a few more. "How about this, Grandma: Lee Morgan."

"Yes, fine."

As I change the record, Grandma continues where she left off. "Dean was my sister's son. Chinsy's third child. She died right after he was born."

"What happened?"

"In those days, after women gave birth they were told to stay in bed. That was the thing to do. They called it bedrest. And she was still on bedrest when something happened, I can't quite remember exactly what..." She trails off and looks down at the floor.

"Well, it's so long ago..."

"But in any case she stood up or got up too quickly to try do something, and must have had a blood clot, or stroke. She died. It was very quick."

"Pretty terrible."

"Those types of things were much more common then."

"So was having such a big family."

"Really, it was almost like Donald and I had a whole bunch of aunts and uncles. Our siblings were almost a generation older than we were. In some ways they were."

"How so?"

"Well, you know my dad fought in the First World War, but Chinsy also left home and went to Edinburgh to nurse. Jean was too young to train as a nurse during the war but still volunteered in the city. And Pat joined the navy. So for them, they'd all been through a world war. The war to end all wars."

"It sounds like you're describing a novel to me or something."

"No, really? You think? I'm sorry to be going on like this. I shouldn't be going on and on." She shakes her head. "I never talk about all this stuff."

"I'm glad you can remember. I don't know much about your family. Did everyone move out to Canada, or did any of them stay in Scotland?"

"We all went out, except for Jean. She'd already married a Scottish fellow. But it wasn't too long after we left that her husband died. So she left Scotland, too. She followed us out to Canada," she says. "Did you ever hear about Chinsy and her husband?"

"No."

"Before Jean married, or any of us children in the family, Chinsy married. She was only eighteen. And she eloped."

"Really? Did that happen a lot back then?"

"No, I don't think so. But yes, she eloped. My parents didn't want her to get married. They told her no. You see, she met this fellow right when the war was breaking out. And he got called up to go over to France. So they decided they would get married before he left."

"See, this sounds like a movie."

"It does a bit, I guess. But it happened. So because he was going off to war, my parents didn't want Chinsy to marry him. They wanted her to wait."

"Why?"

"Because of the war. Who knew what was going to happen? Of course, that was also what made them *want* to marry as soon as possible."

"Yeah, I can see that."

"And she did. That was Chinsy. She actually climbed out her window."

"Come on . . ."

"Yes, he'd put a ladder up to the second floor and off they went. A week later he was off to France."

"And what happened?"

"He lasted a few months before he was killed."

"Unbelievable."

"She remarried in Canada. In fact, Jean and Chinsy married brothers. They were farmers and lived in Saskatchewan."

"Do you remember them, the brothers?"

"Oh, yes. They were hard workers. Neither was born a farmer; they both did it out of necessity. Farming is tough work when it doesn't come naturally. I liked them. I always tried to get along with everyone, I guess. In a family that size, there's always so many different personalities.

So it can be pretty easy for things to get complicated. But we tried to be close. I never had to try hard to be close with Donald. I think because we were so near in age. And because, let's face it, it was Donald. He was always very good to me."

"It seems like you guys all did stuff."

"What do you mean?"

"I'm not sure. It's just, this is interesting for me to hear about your family. Seems like lots of stories there. Lots of intriguing, complicated lives."

"Well, come to think of it, all the women in my family worked. Chinsy was a nurse, Lottie taught primary school, and Della taught at business college. Even my mom worked. She kept the store and rooms. That was our connection with the Old Country. My mom was a businesswoman. She knew what she was doing. It was rare in those days."

"Yeah, see, that's what I mean."

Again the record ends and we're counterintuitively interrupted by lack of music. "What about another?" asks Grandma.

"For sure."

This time I go with Artie Shaw.

11:23 a.m.

WE'VE MADE IT through two more full records. We've been talking less and listening more closely. We've moved from Shaw to Charlie Parker and on to Coleman Hawkins. Grandma has turned the conversation to me. She's commented again about how much she likes my desk and bookcase. She wonders if I had them when I lived in Toronto.

"You had a pretty small place in Toronto, didn't you? A basement apartment?"

"Yup, it was tiny. I didn't have my desk then. It wouldn't have fit."

"Didn't you have a name for it, for your apartment?"

I'm surprised Grandma remembers this. She never saw my Toronto apartment.

"Yeah, I named it the Bunker, on the first day we lived there."

"That's right, the Bunker."

It was the most sensible name for the sunless basement apartment I shared with my girlfriend, Maeve. We'd moved in during the spring of 2006. The entire apartment, including kitchen and bathroom, was similar in size to your average family room — only much smaller, with fewer windows, and with less furniture and no fittings.

"We had to enter through a door at the side of the house. You couldn't see it from the street, Grandma. Our entrance was off an alley.

"The door opened to a staircase. At the bottom were two doors. Laundry machines were on the left. To the right, the Bunker. It had a table for two, and a warming-type instrument that wasn't really a microwave and wasn't really a convection oven but had the worst qualities of each. So most meals were either takeout or cooked on the hot-plate burner built into the counter. There was a dented, lime-stained sink, three cupboards, and a yellow wooden bookcase against the south wall. We also had a lamp."

Grandma seems interested to hear about the Bunker. I haven't shared many of my memories of the apartment or my time there. She's brought her hands together on her lap again, interlocking her fingers. I continue telling her about my old place.

"Oh, and two convenient steps from the kitchen and dining space was our bathroom. For some reason it had a wicker door. Wicker as a bathroom door was definitely creative. You don't usually see that kind of thing. That's because wicker provides as much privacy as chicken wire. Two more steps through a frayed curtain was the bed and dresser.

"The walls of the Bunker were brick painted white and grey, but the first foot or so from the floor was exposed concrete. If it sounds kinda jail-cell-y, it should. It was. After we signed the lease, I told Maeve it just needed a good eye and a human touch to make the place feel a little more homey.

"So I hung two posters with Scotch tape. One was of Andre Agassi leaning on a red Lamborghini, wearing white jeans and his genre-defining mullet. The caption said 'Ace of Hearts.' I'd won the poster after finishing third in a grade six science fair. Agassi lived in the middle of the room, above and to the right of the table. I also put up a creased paper map of eastern Europe from a discarded *National Geographic* I found on the subway. I hung the Eastern Bloc directly above our bed."

"It always helps to have something on the walls," says Grandma.

"The Bunker was too hot in summer and too cold in winter. The spring and fall were better, but in those seasons we had other issues," I explain. "The bugs were worse then."

"You lived there for a while, didn't you?"

"Yeah, we did. And I don't want to give you the wrong idea. It wasn't all bad. It was in the Bunker that I first started cooking. That's when I became a chef."

More accurately it was when I became the Keith Moon of sautéing mushrooms.

"Really, that's when you started? And now you're so good at it."

"I wouldn't say that, Grandma. I enjoy it. It's good to get your mind off other things. But yeah, that's where it started. In those days, I was working a couple days a week for a radio show, so I often worked from home. Maeve worked full-time at a hospital. So while Maeve was helping sick people, I felt I should be doing something, too. When my work wasn't going well, cooking injected my day with some tangible purpose."

"I always liked cooking, too. I know what you mean. Especially when it's for someone else," says Grandma.

"We weren't paying for cable, but for some reason we got the Food Network. It was a channel I'd never watched before."

"I don't think I get that channel at home."

"At first I thought it was boring and deeply inane. But after a couple of weeks I didn't hate it, and after a month or two I started to really get into it. It didn't matter what kind of cooking show it was. I became an addict. I was addicted to the Food Network. Shows with chefs making elaborate meals in thirty minutes were like heroin to me. The ones that were competition-style, pitting chefs against each other with secret ingredients, that was my nicotine."

Marijuana, my marijuana.

"Watching meals being prepared," I continue, "became a strange form of escapism. It blurred reality. There was nothing demanding or difficult about watching these attractive chefs cook, but it felt more like I was learning or improving. When I looked in the mirror, instead of an unpublished bearded writer who spent afternoons listening continuously to a single Vera Lynn record, I saw a real chef coming into his own."

"What kind of dishes did you make? I bet they were pretty fancy."

"I'm not sure I'd say fancy. My first dish was something I called Iain's Exotic Indian. The first time I made it was in September. It's funny, I can still remember it well. It was hot and humid, like summer. The heat made the Bunker feel even smaller. I remember it took ten minutes to slice and wash the onion, green pepper, and mushrooms. It would have been faster had I done it in the proper order, washing the vegetables first.

"Then I uncapped the jar of korma and poured it into the pan. I'd found the korma on sale in the 'exotic' aisle — it was actually called that. It had instructions on the back, which I ignored. Every chef needs some distinction, some personal flair. The mushroom caps I added were my own idea. But once the mushrooms were in, the sauce bubbled up and the entire apartment started to smell like burnt fungus."

"I've always liked mushrooms. I can see why that was your favourite meal."

"In hindsight, it was borderline inedible, Grandma,

really offensive stuff. It's crazy but I really believed it was all right at the time. When Maeve got home from work that night, she was tired and hungry. I kept watching her as we ate. I was waiting for that look of gratitude, or at least enjoyment. Instead, she looked more bored and confused than anything.

"I asked what was wrong. I asked if it was too spicy for her, too daring for her palate. Maeve told me she was just a little confused by mushrooms in korma. I replied something about how hard it was to try and explain cheffy stuff to a non-chef. She also said something about korma being the least daring of any Indian food. I didn't tell her about the other three jars of korma sauce that were waiting for us in the cupboard."

"Well, at least you were trying something new," she says. Grandma's giggling now. "And you've come a long way since then. That was a long time ago."

"Just a few years," I say, "and I haven't really. But at least I have this desk. And a better kitchen."

After I flip the record, we don't talk for a while. I'm still thinking about my years in Toronto, in the Bunker. Grandma is resting back in her chair.

It's fascinating what essential details we forget and which ones we remember with sharp clarity; details that seem paltry when lived but later, with time and perspective, are recalled with a greater relevance.

I'm remembering being in bed the night after the korma incident. By then, after we'd done the dishes, Maeve and I couldn't help but laugh at my string of culinary shipwrecks. We laughed some more, me less heartily. I'd already switched my focus. I'd tossed my book aside and was hunting for the remote. *Iron Chef* was about to start. I had to lean across the still-chortling Maeve to get it. For some reason I just lay there, across and on top of her. I can remember her stomach flexing with each laugh before she finally turned over to go to sleep.

"Do you hear that?" Grandma asks. Neither of us has said anything in a while. We've just been listening to the music, and I assume that's what she's referring to.

"Yeah, it's great, isn't it?" We've listened to another full record.

"No, the music is fine. I don't mean the music, though."

"What?"

"I can hear something else. Is there someone at the door?"

"Shit! I mean, yeah, probably the water guys."

The water guys are standing outside, shoulder to shoulder. Apparently, without warning, the rain has started again. It must be getting close to noon. I'm still in my housecoat. "Sorry, guys, hope you weren't out here long. We were listening to music."

They look surly but unflappable. They're uninterested in my apology or daily log. It's not the first time they've waited at a door, out in the rain. "We're here to look at the hot water tank." They sound surly, too, delivering their remarkably obvious comment.

"Yup, great, come on in." I open the door wide, stepping aside.

The water guys are in that vastly nonspecific age demographic: older than me but younger than Grandma, with plenty of years to choose from. I'm going to guess in their mid-forties. They're both burly, with thick, wide shoulders. One is quite tall, the other short. Along with their goatees, the rest of their uniforms are simple: the colour blue. They aren't wearing anything with a logo or insignia. Just blue sweat tops and dark blue work pants. Did I mention they aren't overly friendly or talkative? This isn't meant as a criticism or insult. I'm fine with it.

I ask if they want any coffee. My offer elicits a sliver of fellowship from the taller one. His face shows signs of acceptance and camaraderie. It's the shorter one who answers for both. He tells me they're good, that they should get started.

They head back outside, collecting a few supplies from their van, and ask if I can show them the tank. Without waiting for an answer, they begin to slip blue covers over their heavy black boots.

No matter how gruff or burly or bushily goateed these repairmen are, their air of machismo dissipates when they slip on those transparent booties over their steel-toed footwear. It has the same effect as if each has a red balloon tied on one wrist while holding a giant rainbow lolly in the other. Boot shower caps help save the carpets, true. They also help make me feel more comfortable around these lads. They level the playing field. I'm in my housecoat and slippers, and they're in their booties.

To get to the hot water tank we have to walk past my room. "How are you doing?" one of them says.

I freeze. Strange, but even offered a bit late, it's nice he's asking. I turn to answer that I'm well and see Grandma waving from her chair. They've stopped with their backs to me and are returning her greeting. The taller one sets down his leather tool satchel.

"Oh, I'm fine, thanks," says Grandma, standing to greet them. "How are you guys? How's work going?"

"Not bad," says the tall one. "Same old." He walks right up to Grandma and puts a large paw on her shoulder with remarkable clemency.

"Nasty weather the last few days, eh," says the shorter one. It's his turn to approach.

"Yup, but it makes it nice for sitting around and getting spoiled."

They laugh, then turn back toward me. Then back to Grandma. I'm certain they don't believe I'm capable of spoiling anyone. "Well, as long as you're comfortable, that's good." The way he says it implies it's directed more at me than her.

"I am," says Grandma. "I am."

"Nice guys, eh?" Grandma says when I get back five or so minutes later. I've left them to their work. They started explaining the issue with the water tank to me. My mind instantly left the furnace room and wandered. I heard them say they'd be able to fix it in no time. That was all I needed/wanted to hear.

"I guess. But did you see their little boot covers? Ridiculous, eh?"

"Oh, I didn't notice."

"Well, they're going to have it all fixed in no time."

"I knew they would," she says confidently. "Here." She passes me two more records. "I picked out a few more while you were gone."

Lionel Hampton is on top. I nod. "We've got nowhere else to be, Grandma. How about some Lionel Hampton?"

"My thought exactly."

1:12 p.m.

AFTER LISTENING TO two more full records, we have some lunch. I make grilled cheese sandwiches with havarti and sliced onion and warm up some soup from yesterday. And I learn something about myself. I'm a worse cook than I think I am. Sometimes I think I'm pretty good, even great. I think I've completely evolved from my early cooking days at the Bunker. But it's at times like these, when I have to make lunch on the fly, with no time to shop, that I buckle and melt bland white cheese between oldish bread.

Grandma seems to like it all right. She says she periodically "craves onions," and she eats everything on her plate. I've offered to drive us downtown so we can get out of my place. Maybe see a little of Kingston. I'm not sure what we're going to do, since the rain is again falling heavily.

En route I suggest we visit a café. We can have something warm to drink somewhere that isn't my kitchen. I sell it as a chance for people-watching. Grandma seems intrigued but tepid.

As we wait for the windshield to defog, I absentmindedly whistle. Grandma pulls some coffee-flavoured candies from her purse and offers me one. I take it, pop it in my mouth, and thank her. She takes one herself. It tastes good, but I wonder if she really wanted one or just wanted me to stop whistling.

I've opted to take the slightly longer, tree-lined route, which curves along Lake Ontario at the base of the university's campus. It's still a short but amply picturesque drive. Usually, anyway. Today it's hard to see much because of the bland colour, drizzle, fog, and steamy windows.

Out of the corner of my eye, I notice Grandma painting the number *1* several times on her foggy window. She uses her index finger like a Magic Marker, cutting through the condensation with her body heat. Something about this lackadaisical doodling makes me think of a scraggy, barefoot prisoner writing out her years on a stone wall in a cell. Thankfully, she stops after four and doesn't cross them with a horizontal fifth.

When I can't find any parking in front of the café, or along the same block, I decide to drop Grandma a few steps from the door. She only has to cross the street. She can duck inside and get us a table. I'll find us a spot on a neighbouring side street. I point to the café a second time and hand my umbrella to her through her open door.

I land a spot a few blocks away that doesn't require me to feed a meter. I'm wet when I get back to the coffee shop. I've jogged so am not soaked, just soggy. I find Grandma inside. She's standing a little hunched, waiting a few steps inside the door, explicitly waterlogged. Her hair is damp; there are a few drips on her forehead. There's a drip on one cheek.

"Grandma, what happened? You're all wet."

Her eyebrow lifts. "Ah, I know, just from coming in from the car," she says. Her raised eyebrow is asking me if I'm a moron: *It's raining, why do you think I'm wet?*

CALGARY
PUBLIC
LIBRARY

September 21, 2019 02:18

39065131101360 12/Oct/2019
The truth about luck : what I learned on my
road trip with grandma (CheckOut)
39065122899212 12/Oct/2019
Pension confidential : 50 things you don't
know about your pension and investments
(CheckOut)

Total 2 Item(s)

"Oh, but what about the umbrella?" Remember? The one I thoughtfully handed to you, the one I didn't get to use?

"It didn't want to open. I tried to get it, but it didn't want to stay open."

"Oh." I could have given her anything. "Sorry." Anything that would have provided some type of shelter: my blue hoodie, a discarded section of newspaper, a post-card would have been opulent in comparison. Instead I've left Grandma with a faulty umbrella that was shitty when brand new. You have to really force it open for it to work.

This will be great for her cold. Just what her doctor would instruct: drink lots of fluids, get some rest, and make sure to stand out in the rain struggling with an unopenable umbrella.

I grab a couple of brown napkins from the dispenser within arm's reach. I start to mop up Grandma's shoulders like she's a yellow Lab fresh off a run through a sprinkler. "Here, sorry about this, Grandma, I should have opened the umbrella for you."

"No, it's fine. It's only my jacket that's wet. And scarf." And head, face, body, and feet.

"Your shoes and pants are a bit wet, too." I kneel down and started wiping off her shins.

We're creating a stir. The baristas are looking at us. So are the customers in line. Even people with headphones seated at tables are turning to watch our performance. I stand up and pause, which gives Grandma enough time to grab a pile of her own napkins. Now she starts to dry *my* shoulders. She has to stand on her toes to reach.

"Thanks, Grandma, but don't worry about me. I'm fine."

"Well, I'm fine, too. It's just a bit of rain."

We move over to the counter like drowned rats. "You can grab a table, Grandma, and I'll get us our drinks."

"Okay," she says.

I ask her what kind of drink she wants, hot or cold? Hot. Tea or coffee? Tea, great. What kind of tea? She takes a step after each question, assuming it's the last.

"Anything is fine, dear," she says over her dewy shoulder. "How about green?"

I turn back to the barista, who's been following our discourse. She's already reaching for a bag of green tea with jasmine. "Exactly," I stammer. "Thanks."

I get myself a coffee. The tea is served in a pot. I carry it along with our mugs over to a table for two in the middle of the café. I sit down with a sigh and unzip my hoodie. Grandma's coat is hanging on the back of her chair.

"Smells good," she says. "I'm about ready for some tea."

I rub my hands together, leaning in over my mug, enjoying the scent and warmth.

There are three large windows facing Princess, one of Kingston's main streets. The tables along the windows are all taken. So are the two large upholstered chairs. Our small table for two is in the middle of the large room, which has a worn hardwood floor. The tables directly to our right and left are occupied. We're wedged in. I could easily touch our neighbours if I raised my arms.

"Is this all right, Grandma? It's busier than I would have thought."

"Fine, dear. I haven't been out to a coffee shop, or café, in . . . I don't know how long."

"Well, good."

I notice a drop or two on her cheek that she still hasn't wiped away. She must not feel it. She leans in across the table. "I can't believe all the computers."

Sometimes the passing of days, months, and years feels illusory. Certain places make it feel like we've stepped into wet, sticky cultural mud, like our feet have been stuck for twenty-odd years. I feel this at fairs, strolling among couples with stuffed pink bears and teenagers nibbling on candy floss and hot dogs.

I think the opposite is probably the case for Grandma in a café. She probably feels as if, by stepping through the doors, she's leaped directly into a year or era she's not even part of, like she's just visiting.

"You're right," I say. "Lots of computers."

In this café Grandma has virtually been reduced to an infant. There's lots for her to look at, but most of it doesn't make a lot of sense to her, and she needs help ordering her drink. Her eyes wander as she fiddles with her mug.

The café relies disproportionately on the natural light flooding in from the windows. There's very little today, which renders all the computer screens brighter; they light up the faces of their owners like personal tanning beds.

Grandma's enthralled by all the machines. She's looking from one to the next and the next. For me it's the people *without* a computer who are intriguing. I've brought a clementine with me and have peeled it. I'm not quite ready to eat it yet, so I use the peel as a biodegradable plate where it can rest.

There's a woman about my age. She's one of the few without a laptop. Instead she has a child, a (real) baby. She also has a friend at the table. The baby looks only a few months old. He keeps reaching up to her from his plastic carrying-crib thingy. With every third or fourth swipe she glances down and makes an extremely silly face. She contorts her face like a pro, like she's been doing it for years. She does it not unaffectionately, without interrupting her discussion. She's so casual and unworried. Yet this child, like all of them, is nightmarishly dependent.

I wonder if she would ever leave this child out in the rain?

"Do you ever bring your computer here?" wonders Grandma.

"Sometimes, yeah. But my battery doesn't seem to last too long."

"I probably should have learned about computers and email and all that. But I just never thought I'd be around long enough to use it. That's a whole world I know very little about."

We sip from our mugs. I eat my first two sections of clementine and offer some to Grandma. She accepts two of her own.

There's an elderly, but not old, man sitting at what I consider to be the worst table. It's closest to the bathroom, within carshot. Not the ideal vicinity in a store that slings highly caffeinated products. I've seen this same man at that table before. He looks like he's part of the chair he's sitting on, like his limbs are made of wood and his skin fabric. He's petrifying at the table before our eyes.

"Such nice windows they have here. Is that a bakery across the street?"

"Yup, they have brilliant bread and monstrous cinnamon rolls."

Grandma usurps my host role and refills her cup from the silver pot. We've spent the morning talking, rehashing memories. Both of us now seem more content to sit quietly. I ask Grandma if she wants a section of the paper. She says no, it's okay. She's probably already read it, this morning before I woke up.

So we just sit and sip and watch and sip and think. We sip perpetually.

Another man to our left, alone, is reading a copy of the *National Post*. He has a slender build and looks to be about fifty. He's a fairly standard-issue middle-aged white fellow. But what's most curious is his choice of eyewear. He's sporting squash goggles.

I want to turn my chair and just stare at him, observe this creature reading his paper. I'd like to follow him around for a day, seriously, just to see what his story is. But I have to show restraint. So I try to be discreet.

My theory: these particular goggles are prescription. He probably lost or broke his regular glasses. He's a professor, the absent-minded sort, and his glasses are probably imbedded in a stack of papers waiting to be marked. He almost certainly spent the morning yelling at his wife for picking up his glasses and putting them down somewhere. I bet he really let her have it. Left without any other options, he went to his gym bag, fished out his sweaty old protective specs, left his house without saying goodbye, and is now trying them out at the café before class. He's also feeling bad that he hasn't been playing squash in a while; it's been months.

He feels out of shape and is now likely regretting the generous splash of cream he put in his coffee.

I eat the rest of my orange and peer around the café. No one else seems to care. Maybe it's because they're all focused on their screens. Even Grandma, who is now consulting her watch wearily.

I'm trying not to listen to two women three tables over. One must be a manager here. I believe the other is vying for casual employment. The younger one is wearing a lined coat. I wish she would take it off. I feel hot just looking at her.

The managerish one is conducting a spontaneous yet weirdly formal interview that switches between friendly dialogue and scripted questions concerning the younger's best and worst personality traits. She's referencing some papers, perhaps a resumé. If I hear the questions I won't be able to help myself from answering. I'm disturbingly aware that this twenty-year-old redhead with fake fingernails would be a more suitable staff member than I'd be. She was just asked what makes her a good team player. Best to ignore. Interviews are always such an artificial, misrepresentative dynamic. What can anyone really glean from such broad, depthless, slogany questions?

I look down into my mug. The cream has separated. I hope this doesn't mean it's gone off. Did I just consume spoiled cream? The whitest part of the cream has formed a map of Iceland, including striking detail of the western fjords. I try to locate the places I visited last time I was there. And with a few clockwise swirls of the cup, a new map is formed, or an animal, or a polygonal shape I don't recognize.

Norman (what I'm now calling the goggled prof) is blowing his nose. I mean really blowing it, for all he's worth. It's absolutely revolting. I didn't mind him when he was just the brilliant but misunderstood experimental physics genius prone to losing his temper. Now that he's content to spread his germs to everyone else, I find him unsightly. You'd think he was trying to loosen and liquify part of his left hemisphere and banish it through his nostrils.

A comment from Grandma turns my head. "Great phone," she says. "I like how it flips open and shut like that. It's amazing."

I've been flipping my phone open and shut subconsciously, neurotically. "Yeah, that's what it's called, Grandma, a flip phone. If you can believe it, they were actually somewhat cool in 2005."

"I *can* believe it. It's quite stylish."

"Yeah, it's okay," I say, looking closely at the phone for the first time in months.

"What can it do? I keep reading about phones nowadays and all the stuff they can do."

"Yeah, I guess it's pretty crazy now what phones can do." I pause. "But yeah, mine can't do a whole lot. I mean, it can call. It can send and receive text messages. It can tell time." And it flips!

"Ah, I see."

The baby in the plastic mini-perambulator yawns. I'm looking at him but still can't believe he's that small. The yawn engulfs his face. Grandma brings her hands together. "Have I ever told you about Marge and Molly?"

"No, I don't think so."

"They were my friends. It was the three of us who signed up together."

"Signed up? For what?"

"The war," she says. "I'm not sure about the other two, but I guess it wasn't really a decision for me. It was inevitable and necessary. It was what I wanted to do."

"How come?"

"My younger brother, Donald, had gone, so I would, too — that was my thinking. He'd lied and enlisted in the air force at sixteen. I hadn't seen him in years. I didn't know where he was. He was so young when he left. I thought about him every day."

I've stopped playing with my phone. I set it down on the table beside the orange peel.

"And to be honest, I wanted to see things. I thought the whole thing would just be an adventure. I guess I was still looking for adventures back then."

My feeling is that Grandma will leave it here if I don't encourage her. But I want to know more. This is a cable of memory that's been buried but from the sound of it is mostly intact. I ask about the days before she left. She tells me they didn't know what to expect. All they knew was that they would be trading relative inaction for action. Winnipeg to Europe. She'd grown up in Winnipeg. It was all she'd known. They didn't know where they were going, or for how long, or what they would find.

"The way they enforced the age for soldiers was pretty lax," she says. "Whereas nurses were held to a strict standard. Nurses had to be twenty-five before they could go."

In the context of soldiers and that war, twenty-five was mature. It was old.

"First we were sent to a staging area. I was asked if I had a preference. Was there somewhere specific I wanted to go? I'd heard of No. 5 hospital. No. 5 was made up almost entirely of nurses and doctors from Winnipeg—I figured I might know some of them. It was the only hospital I knew anything about. My two chums had been unsure where to go. I told them about No. 5 over tea one afternoon."

"Where was No. 5?"

"It had been set up just outside London. So that's where the three of us decided to go."

"And then you were gone?"

"Yup, it felt like it all happened quite quickly. My family left our tiny fishing village in Scotland and moved to Canada when I was two. I'd never been back to Scotland, or Europe, since. I hadn't done any travelling. That first trip to Canada was the only time I'd ever sailed the Atlantic or been on a boat. I was too young to form any conscious memories of that trip. But from what my mother used to tell me, it was a gentle trip aboard a typical commuter ship."

"So this was your second transatlantic journey, but it felt like your first."

"We were just thrilled to be moving. I also found it wasn't only nurses travelling but soldiers, too. The ship was smaller than I'd expected. It was a cruise ship in peacetime and had been commandeered for the war.

"Our cabin was more than adequate: two sets of bunks and some drawers to share. I didn't find sea life all that bad.

Marge and Molly weren't so lucky. They were pretty seasick. Most of the nurses and soldiers were pretty sick."

"Yeah, that makes sense. You guys weren't sailors."

"Just shows how lucky I was. I never even lost my appetite. I loved my time on the decks, watching the sea in front and the foamy salt water we'd cut through and left behind. We were finally sailing. I was among friends. I was around strangers. We were heading to London."

Grandma tells me her evenings on the ship were generally absorbed at the ship's bar. Even at night, she liked the decks best. She liked the air. Some nights she would walk outside alone. More typically she was joined by others.

Those seasick souls were also seeking the fresh air. Others just couldn't sleep. Some were "feeling their drink." Some just wanted to sit and talk.

As Grandma recounts her time on the ship, it sounds to me like it had the mood of a migrating slumber party, not a war-bound crusade. They talked of nothing in particular. No one knew what was to come, and they probably talked more about what they were leaving than where they were going. Grandma was comfortable and content spending time alone, but solitude would be rare in the months to come.

"When we finally reached the continent, staging began at Taplow, a village on the east bank of the River Thames. We were billeted in rooms in a small house on the grounds of a stately manor. The doctors and surgeons of the hospital were close by, but in different buildings. I can still remember how lovely the estate grounds were. But luckily for the three of us, we didn't need to spend every day at the estate.

We were so close to London. And we went into the city every chance we got. We'd all heard so much about London."

"What was London like in those days?" I'm trying to keep my questions brief. Grandma has been ignoring her tea, and I'm sensing she is on a roll.

"Well, we were never alone, but always in groups. Soldiers, mostly American and British, were everywhere. Children on the street weren't unheard of, but it was rare. Mostly I remember a city of young people. We'd go to shows and pubs amidst the buzz-bomb warnings and sirens. Once we were stranded in a theatre while watching a movie. A bomb had struck nearby and we were forced to wait inside the theatre until the all-clear was given. When it finally came, instead of leaving, we kept watching the movie; we had to know how it was going to end."

I look around me, at the other tables and people in the café. Everyone is busy with their computers and books, their music and papers. I have the urge to tell everyone to shut up, to gather around, to listen. But I don't.

Grandma continues. It was a few months post-arrival that she was granted her first leave. She put in her request, assuming, like her friends, it would be accepted. It wasn't. She was called to see the colonel in his office. He was perplexed. Why did she want to spend her very first leave in the north of Scotland? He told her it wouldn't be possible. There was a large naval base in the area. Access was restricted.

"I stayed in his office listening to his ruling, but I was disappointed. I decided to tell him why I wanted to go. I was *from* Wick. I still had family there, family I hadn't seen in years. I'd never been back and had never been this close. When he heard the whole story, he immediately agreed. He granted me permission to go back to my hometown.

"When all my uncles, aunts, and cousins saw me, no one in Wick could believe it was me. They were really surprised. They hadn't seen me since I was two. Now I was twenty-five. I guess they just never imagined I'd be back in the village. And they really got a kick out of seeing my nurse's uniform.

"When I got back to Taplow, it was right back into routine. We were on strict rations. I hadn't seen an egg since arriving. Butter and cream were very hard to come by. Cheese, my very favourite, was completely unavailable. It was my relatives who I'd visited who started sending me packages. Had it been non-wartime, those packages would have seemed quite modest. During this time, the content was indulgent. Every month I would receive a small parcel with a dozen eggs and a pound of butter. You can't imagine how good those eggs tasted.

"The hospital at Taplow was full, it was over capacity. I'd been assigned to ward duties, mostly on the recovery floors, looking after patients who were on the mend. My next assignment was to the officers' ward. There was one particular American officer I got to know better than most. He was a dedicated smoker; he preferred cigars to cigarettes. He was badly burned from an explosion and couldn't light his own. Twice a day I would visit him. He would lie there, smoking, and I would linger in the cloud beside the bed. We would talk. Mostly he would talk, I would listen. He would tease me, though, saying, 'You've been so kind since the baby came.'"

I'm not entirely sure what it means, but Grandma laughs aloud at the memory.

"Others times he wouldn't talk much. We would sit in silence. You don't get that anymore in cafés or anything, the smoke. Which I guess is for the best. It never really bothered me, though. I kinda liked the smell. I probably still do."

"Do you remember my smoking phase, my early infatuation with smoking?"

"Yes, right. You and your smoking. I'd completely forgotten about that. It was so funny. You really wanted to smoke and took it so seriously."

"Yeah, I did." I sigh. "I loved everything about it, even the smell. Or I thought I did. And Mom's theory was if she really tried to discourage me, I'd probably find it more appealing. So she was happy to go along with it."

"I can remember you always wanted to sit in the smoking sections of restaurants."

"Don't remind me. I was about four years old at the time. When we had guests over, I'd always have my unlit cigarette with me. I would exhale spurts of perfectly clean air throughout the room and ask if it was too smoky for them. I was completely ridiculous."

"Didn't you also have an empty pack to hold it in?"

"Exactly. At that point it really felt like my world was complete. It was my very first prized possession. It was like if someone gave me my own home today."

"And wasn't it your mom's idea to cut up the straws?"

"Yes, exactly. A week after I got the cigarette, she thought my pack looked empty. She offered to fill it with plastic straws cut to the same length. She said it would feel full and look real. It did."

"Anytime we came to visit, you had that pack with you. It was like your version of a ratty old teddy bear."

"I know," I say, shaking my head, "so strange. Whenever company — and not just family but whoever — was coming over, I'd position myself in my favourite armchair, which faced the front door. I'd have a book in my lap and set up my ashtray and place my real cigarette between my fingers. I'd studied the way Grandpa smoked and knew the technique. I never held it firmly, but as if I'd forgotten it was even there. I'd wait for the guests to arrive."

Grandma tilts the last of her tea into her mouth. She sets her cup down and shakes her head. "You see, I was going on so much, my tea is ice cold."

I follow and drain what's left of my coffee. It's also cold. "No, no, it was me going on. I'm glad you told me that stuff. That's why we came out here, to chat."

"But not just about my old memories," she says. "All those things happened so long ago. I'm not sure what got me started on all that."

Despite being full, the café feels empty. Each person sits in their own invisible cocoon. I don't feel like staying any longer. I suddenly want to leave.

"Well, what do you think, Grandma, shall we?" I ask.

"We shall."

The lady with her baby is up and ready to go. His tiny eyes are red and watery. His thin hair, still very blond, is matted down in the front but standing up straight in the back. It's classic baby bed-head. His mother cradles him in one arm now, rocking him slowly and sweetly.

I help Grandma with her coat. Out of the corner of my eye I watch the young mother use caution as she zips her son's coat up. His eyes have closed and she's extra careful when she gets the zipper right up under his chin.

2:39 p.m.

A GREYNESS HAS settled onto everything. All is drab. My town has become an overused washcloth that hangs over a faucet — damp and dingy and tired. It's not just the sky but the streets, the buildings, people's faces. This feels like a new, undesired season, something in between winter and spring.

It's too brisk to be shopping outdoors, but I haven't been to a farmers' market since last fall. I don't want to take Grandma back to my apartment yet. I've dragged her out in this weather, and it'll take at least one more stop before I can justify this as an outing.

We have a small but bountiful market in Kingston. All the fresh foodstuffs anyone needs, packed into the square behind city hall. During the winter, Market Square is converted into a public skating rink. And one night a week in the summer, the square is transformed into an outdoor movie theatre where everyone is encouraged to show up at dusk with a lawn chair and watch a classic film on the massive screen. For a small city, the downtown square gets a lot of use. This time of year, though, the square still has a foot in winter and the other not yet firmly planted in spring. The farmers' market won't be in full swing for another few weeks.

I have an alternative plan. There's another market, a smaller one, on the university campus on Wednesdays. In a pinch, it will do. And I'm in a pinch.

We park on the campus, beside the main library. We do one lap around the outside of the market at a snail's pace. Even for Grandma we're moving slowly, heavily. We've bought nothing. I've squeezed a loaf of Portuguese bread. Grandma has commented on the man selling Russian snacks, something about it smelling good. I hope she's at least enjoying the stroll and the relatively fresh air.

I stop in front of the fresh veggie stand. They can't be local, not yet. They're probably the same ones I've been buying in the grocery store, grown in a greenhouse. Somehow they look more appetizing on display outside on a wobbly folding table.

Grandma is a couple of steps behind me. A quick shoulder-check confirms she's concerning herself with the flower lady. The flower stall held my attention for about three seconds. I robotically reach out and pick up a tomato. I'm about to release it when the lady working the stall looks up from her chair. She's not really a lady, more a young, curvaceous woman of about my own age. I suppose I don't *need* to drop this tomato just yet.

There's something I find, I don't know, appealing about her. Maybe it's that she's attractive and around my age. And also that I've been spending all my time with a ninety-two-year-old to whom I'm directly related. I pause, examine, and then bring the red fruit up to my face. I give the tomato a sniff and nod my approval.

"A nice piece of fruit," I say.

"Yeah, they're ripe," she says, standing up. Okay, this *is* an attractive woman. And an entrepreneur to boot.

"I've always enjoyed tomatoes, even as a young kid," I say, sniffing it again, this time longer. "They've gotta be one of my favourite things, like, in general." In general? I need to stop sniffing this tomato.

"Well, they're a pretty good price, too."

See, she knows about prices and economic theory. She's not just a pretty face. "I use them for loads of things. Sauces, sandwiches...you name it..."

She smiles, but her eyes dart toward the ground. Predictably, I'm losing her. I hear Grandma sneeze behind me. I turn and instinctively pull her into me. I softly set my left arm around her shoulders. I've been noticing today that when Grandma and I walk around, people take a good, long look at us. They look much longer than when it's just me walking alone, when I can be invisible. And they aren't looking in a malicious way. I think they think she's cute or something. I think they think it's noble of me to be spending time with this little old lady.

It also helps that I've been holding up an umbrella (no one else knows it's mostly useless) for both of us but am clearly favouring her. *My* left shoulder is wet. My entire left side is wet. People like this kind of thing. They think I'm a good, charitable guy. The assumption is chivalry. When we walk down the street, as long as I'm holding the umbrella with my left hand over Grandma, I could be swinging a two-day-old puppy by its tongue with my right hand, à la set of keys, and these people would still find the scene charming.

"Grandma," I yell, pulling her in even closer, bending down to eye level, "are you okay? Don't worry, everything's fine, we're still at the market." I peer up at the girl. She's noticed Grandma.

Grandma shoots me a stern look. "Yes, I know. I'm fine. Hello," she says to the girl.

"Hi there."

"I'm just out with my Grandma," I say. "I think it's good for her to be out in the fresh air. She's ninety-two, after all."

"What, really? You're ninety-two!?"

"Pardon me?" says Grandma.

"She was just wondering how old you are, Grandma," I shout directly into her face. "She can't believe you are the age you are." I look back to the girl, my arm squishing Grandma into my side. "I think our little walks really help."

And with that a man, clearly both a legitimate farmer and her boyfriend/husband, appears from somewhere to the left carrying a large brown box. He sets it down and starts unpacking jars of something. Probably jam. His arms are strong and veiny.

"I guess you guys just buy that from the store or something, right?" I say.

"Nope, we grow the fruit, make the jam, and jar it ourselves," he says.

"Cheaper than the store, too," she says.

"Oh, it does look nice, doesn't it?" says Grandma.

"Well... I'm not much of a jam guy, Grandma..."

"Are you sure? I don't mind buying us a jar."

I've already moved a few steps back toward the car.

"Come on, Grandma. I think I can feel the rain coming again."

"Okay, but we just have to wait for something. I hope that's okay."

"Oh, sure. What?"

"I bought some flowers at that stall back there. They're making me a special bouquet."

While we wait, I see a young mother and baby. At first I think it's the same ones from the café. Then I don't think it is. This baby is crying, which seems out of character for the placid lad I knew at the café. The mother is unfazed by the crying. I think it might be the worst sound in the world. Maybe I'm just feeling irritable. I can't imagine getting used to it, though. I ask Grandma.

"I know how it seems. But things change when the kids are your own," she says.

"Yeah, I guess." I realize a moment later she didn't really answer my question. Or maybe she did.

"Oh, look," she says, tapping my shoulder, "the flowers are ready. And they're beautiful."

7:12 p.m.

WE SPENT THE rest of the afternoon alone. Not only from others but from each other. Grandma in the pink chair, with her book and tea. Me at my desk, in my room. I've been at my desk for a while. Now I decide to just lie down on the floor. I stay like this, stationary, supine on the floor, for ten minutes. Then twenty. Then half an hour.

I wonder how long Grandma is going to live?

It's not something I've ever seriously considered before today. I've thought about it, but always in the context of how long she's *already* lived. She's lived so long, through so many years, eras. But I haven't thought about looking ahead, at how long she has left. She can't have much time left. What becomes the priority at that point in life, looking back or ahead? When your days are numbered, do you think of much else?

If I were ninety-two I would be wrestling with these questions often. Maybe daily. Maybe hourly. Only in old, old age are we objectively certain our time is almost up. Death is life's only inevitability (yeah, taxes, I know, I know). Is the fear of death more about ourselves or losing others? There seems to be a link between physical discomfort, pain, and death, but when we die, it likely hurts those closest to us more than us. But really we know nothing about death beyond the obvious. What does that say about existence, that we understand very little (apart from conflicting theories) about its only absolute? I'm still lying on the floor when Grandma knocks on the door. She has something with her. It's the flowers from the market. She thinks I could use them in my room.

"But they're your flowers, Grandma. You bought them. You love flowers."

"They'll look good in here," she says.

I could ask her about the things I've been thinking about, about death. But I don't. Not yet, anyway. I don't want her to think about it if she doesn't. And I don't want her to think I'm grilling her. Just because she's closer to the end of life doesn't mean anything. And I suppose she isn't necessarily closer to the end anyway. That's the perception, the likelihood, but it's not a certainty. She's definitely close, but maybe I'm closer.

"Remember what you were telling me at the café? About being in Taplow?"

"Yes, all that talk has got me thinking more this afternoon. That's what I've been doing. I wasn't reading much at all, just thinking. I've been in my head a lot today. More than usual for me."

"Did you stay there long? In Taplow, I mean?"

"Well, the day our routine finally changed I think it was a grey, rainy day. I don't know why I think that. After breakfast all the nurses were brought together and told we would begin marching drills, rain or shine. We weren't told why, or for how long. We were generally told little. That morning, what I felt was closest to excitement. I knew what it likely meant, to be drilling. I'd been anticipating a change in our activities. It would mean another move."

"Did you know where?"

"No, dear. But luckily, I'd always been a walker, even back while studying. I didn't mind the marching drills. It was written in my high school yearbook that I was the fastest walker in the school. On our morning marches, if the mist wasn't too thick, we could see Windsor Castle.

"The morning drills weren't the only change. We started participating in mandatory gas training. Nothing had been confirmed but nothing had been denied. All we knew was something was imminent. They even had us going to lectures on tropical medicine. A couple of weeks later, the oldest nurses and any in poor health were sent back to Canada. No. 5 had been picked. As we all figured, we were moving."

"And you were fine with that, just having everything change without warning?" It's a stupid question considering the context, and I realize this as I ask it.

Grandma laughs it off. "Oh, sure. That's what we'd signed up for."

I decide I should ask fewer questions and just listen.

"Since leaving Canada I'd been sleeping less. Not because I couldn't sleep — I can always sleep — but sleeping seemed out of place, almost like I thought it should be rationed, too. There was too much work and activity. London had been fun."

She tells me the story again, the one she told me at the café, about the bombing when she was at the movie (she does repeat herself, like any ninety-two-year-old would). She'd enjoyed her time but still considered it good news they were moving again. They were closer to the action than they'd been in Winnipeg, but she wanted to be closer still, to be part of it.

"My biggest regret was that I never did get to see Donald while in England."

It seems so irrational to me, unlikely, that this would have ever happened. But she tells me this twice, that she'd really believed she might see him. London would have been her best chance. She'd had a feeling on the boat that she was going to see him. It was a mightily implausible hope. It was confirmed, three weeks after arriving in England, just how unlikely.

"I received word Donald had been shot down. Again. This time somewhere in northern Africa."

She was glad she was busy and that she had people to care for, depending on her.

"There were so many rumours during our last days at Taplow. Everyone had their own ideas. Our destination was a closely guarded secret, and of course I was curious but knew it was outside my control. No one knew for sure, not even the soldiers or officers.

"Even after boarding the ship we didn't know. I spent even less time in my cabin on this voyage. I knew even more people now than on the trip over. I still liked the decks at night. We would chat in groups, about lots of things, some theorizing about where we were going."

"You still weren't sure?"

"No. Some of the officers tried to use the stars as a map. We all started to detect a very slight warming in temperature, or thought we did, and figured we must be going south. When we passed through Gibraltar, things became clearer, and then finally we knew when we anchored at our final destination."

"Where?"

"We were in Sicily. We'd landed at Augusta as part of the Allied convoy. The morning we landed we were immediately sent down below. You see, we were landing with the invading troops and were under heavy fire. There were some serious injuries, but it was actually our supply ship that took the brunt of the shelling. We lost our medical supplies and even our uniforms. To disembark we had to climb down rope ladders fastened to the side of the ship. I can still see us. I was wearing my silk stockings, a nurse's cap, and a knee-length skirt, and over the side we went."

"That's unbelievable."

"The British officers were aghast. They couldn't believe these Canadian nursing sisters, these women, had landed with an invading force in an active war zone. It was unheard of."

"I guess you must have felt part of it all after that."

"We certainly did. Everything, the mood, our duties, it all changed after that. No. 5's new home was an abandoned generic two-storey building we converted into a makeshift hospital. It had been booby-trapped by the Nazis before they fled. We were told to be very careful with everything; toilet seats could explode when lifted, even a single pen could be hazardous. We had no supplies and very little equipment.

"Our clothes had also sunk with the supply ship. The nurses were given men's army uniforms to wear. They didn't fit any of us. We would laugh and tease one another about who looked the worst in the baggy pants. But the hospital became active and hectic right away. There was no time for further training or practice. It was time to work. We cared for patients all day or all night or both. On one occasion, while changing the dressings of a badly wounded American soldier, I found a nest of maggots underneath the old bandages. I didn't say anything to the patient, but I left them. They would all fall off eventually, when their helpful work was done."

"Was the hospital full?"

"It was. It was well over capacity. We had to line up any extra cots in hallways, anywhere there was space. Lots of dysentery and malaria. The badly wounded who weren't sent back to England were contained on the top floor. The first floor was reserved for the sick, infirm, and less seriously injured. More sick, wounded, and maimed arrived daily. Amputations became ordinary. So did surgeries of all kinds. I always thought it was the night that was hardest on the boys.

"The bombings that had sunk the supply ship continued. You could hear the planes flying overhead. The shelling was focused on the harbour, but the blasts were felt and heard throughout the hospital. At their peak I would just walk up and down the aisles, in between the beds and cots. I wouldn't talk. I just felt like I had to do something, that maybe even my presence might be a help. I hoped it offered some comfort, a sense of composure."

"Yeah," I say, "it would have."

There's no music playing now, no radio or TV on. My room is very quiet.

"And then again it was time for No. 5. to move. We proceeded to Catania, a larger city at the base of Mount Etna. It wasn't until our third day at Catania that I was off duty for an entire afternoon, and I was recruited to play in a rugby match organized by a group of British soldiers. I'd met them the day before. It was my first time playing rugby. I tried not to let on. I'd missed playing sports. I enjoyed it. It was fun to get out and play something again. Now why do I remember that?"

I'm finding that these tangents in her stories are some of my favourite parts. There's much she's forgotten, so there must be some reason these moments have lodged themselves in her consciousness. They seem to come out of nowhere, as if she's surprising herself with them.

Grandma saw what you see when you're part of war, when you're living it every day, when an earlier reality is overhauled and rebuilt as something unfamiliar. Sights that were previously unimaginable were made reliably probable.

"I'd been tending to a patient who arrived with a badly broken leg when there was a ruckus outside. I went out with the other nurses on duty. Not far down the road, a procession was coming toward the hospital. There was lots of commotion. They were loud, emotional. It wasn't obvious if they were angry or distressed.

"As they got closer I could see they were very upset. There were men and women. There were children. They were all weeping, calling out toward the hospital. They had a wooden wagon. Inside the wagon was a middle-aged Sicilian man. A farmer. He'd been out working, plowing his fields or planting. It was uncertain what he'd been doing, but while he was doing it, he'd hit a mine.

"The group was asked to wait outside. The farmer was removed from the wagon and brought in. Once in the operating room, I knew from the number and severity of the injuries that nothing could be done. It wasn't long after arriving that he died."

"I guess in a weird way it would have been worse when it was something like that," I say. "When it was just a family and a farmer."

"I was lucky I didn't see more of that type of thing. That one sticks out in my mind because of the family being there, I think..."

For a while we don't talk. Then I ask Grandma if she's hungry. She wonders if we should go back and try the restaurant that was closed yesterday. As I get my jacket on, Grandma remembers her initial reason for coming to my room. She'd almost forgotten the flowers. She suggests I put them on top of my bookshelf.

That way, she thinks, I can see them from anywhere in the room.

8:11 p.m.

"I HAVEN'T THOUGHT about this in years. I really haven't."

We've just had our first sips of Chianti. It was Grandma's idea when we sat down in this booth. We didn't have to wait to be seated. We dashed in from the car (Grandma was our pacer, so *dash* might not be the most accurate verbiage). It was her idea to leave the umbrella, despite the rain.

It's a different type of grape, but the wine is having the same effect as last night. It's rendered her into a talkative, nostalgic Grandma. Or maybe it's all the talking we've done today already. I'm still thrown by this. I often go days without use of my vocal cords, and Grandma's default position is firmly set in listening mode. She's usually asking about others but rarely is the one to talk about herself, to tell her own stories. To be honest, I didn't know she had many.

Combined with her tenacious sense of humour and ability to tease, Grandma's default setting, when I was growing up, was to sit and ask questions about what each of us was up to. She wanted to know what was keeping us busy. She wanted to hear what was happening at school or how my basketball team was doing. She wanted to look over any recent photographs, asking about faces she didn't recognize. She always remembered the names of any of my friends she'd met, and she would ask about them.

The terrain of adolescence shapes an inadvertently one-sided relationship. The proper footing of reciprocation was too tricky and developed. I would share all of the trivialities of my day but never ask about hers. The only kid who would sit and ask their elderly grandparents about the details of their lives in an attempt to better understand them would be a character from a Wes Anderson film. We understood Grandma through her reaction to our stories. It was her receptivity to our existence that formed her identity. We, the young unintentional solipsists, would talk; Grandma would listen and react. That was her way.

"Well, that's good, I'm happy to chat about these things," I say. "Have a bit more."

I top up her glass, even though there's no room for topping. It's more a symbolic gesture, I suppose.

The atmosphere in here is a blend of pub and family restaurant. Probably 60/40 in favour of pub. But the patrons are probably 60/40 in favour of families. There is a large bar on one side of the room and booths along the walls. Tables of varying sizes fill in the rest. You wouldn't call it fancy, but the expectation is for large portions of comfort food. It's mostly full tonight. The music, laughter, talking has created an auditory fog of white noise around us.

"Did you know I love sports?"

"Well, I know you like watching hockey, Grandma."

"But I mean I love *playing* sports."

"Yeah, I knew you played tennis and curled. And that rugby game you played overseas. And you still play golf, right?"

"Yup. But it just wasn't as easy back in my day."

"Really?"

"I can remember being in Winnipeg in the twenties. In the winter there were outdoor rinks all over. The girls were supposed to just skate around while the boys played hockey. That's just the way it was. Can you imagine? I hated that."

"You wanted to play hockey?"

"Of course. It's silly for you to think about it today, but I found it ridiculous to think about it then, too. They didn't want me to play, because I was a girl. So obviously I played."

"With other girls?"

"No, I couldn't find any other girls to play, or boys, either. It wasn't really done, I don't think. But I got Donald to play with me. He agreed to be my goalie. We'd have to go to the rink early in the morning, before school, when no one else was there, and I would just skate up and down and shoot pucks at him. We were always alone out there, and it was very quiet at that time of day. You could hear the skates cutting through the ice, but that was about it. When I think about it, he never complained. He knew I loved playing. He was very good to me."

"Yeah, you guys got on pretty well, didn't you?"

"We did. But everyone got on well with Donald. He was just... that way. He was so easygoing, very accepting of everyone. When we were young, we'd agreed that if either of us ever had any kids, we'd name them after each other."

"Do you think he enjoyed playing?"

"Oh, sure, I think so. I'd score on him more often than not, though. I don't think he liked that. And he wasn't letting me, either," she says, leaning back in her chair. "I had a pretty good shot." Remembering her trash-bin shot this morning, I believe her.

"And in high school, I was the female sports captain. I think some of the girls would have been embarrassed by that title. I liked it. And truth be told, I had my eye on the male captain. He was the best athlete in the school, but not cocky. He was quiet." She laughs. "He never really noticed me, though."

I smile. I don't want to get her off track, but the waitress is lurking. She wants to take our order. We haven't even opened our menus yet.

"Why don't you order for both us?" says Grandma. "I think you know what I like by now."

Yes, I do. She likes everything. "Okay," I say.

I order a margherita pizza and some sweet potato fries on the side. I've seen a couple of pizzas come out of the kitchen. It appears to be high-quality wheel.

"I knew by high school what I wanted to do," Grandma continues when the waitress leaves with our order. "But the thing was, by the time I finished high school, well, I was still too young to get in."

"Get in where?"

"Winnipeg General. I wanted to be a nurse. I knew it even then."

"So what did you do?"

"I wasn't sure what to do. That was all I wanted. But my

mother didn't want me sitting around and waiting. So she decided I should sign up for business classes."

"Really?"

"Yup, my sister Della was teaching the classes. It wasn't long after I started studying there that I became of age and was accepted to the hospital."

"And how long was the nursing program?"

"It was going to be for three years. Of course my first roommate only made it through three months and then she was gone. There was a lot to learn, and I remember we had a very demanding instructor in our first year. A lot of the students didn't get along with her."

"Did you like her?"

"I didn't have any problems with her. Well, except once. She caught me sleeping on a shift. I was working in the baby ward during the overnight shift and was exhausted. I think I'd been out to a dance the night before. Anyhow, I figured it wouldn't hurt to just sit down for a few minutes and close my eyes."

"And you got caught?"

"I was sitting up but using my cap as a pillow and I must have really dozed off, because I was woken up by the instructor's voice saying my name. That's all she said, but she said it loudly and with anger. Some of the other girls thought I was done for, but she never mentioned it again. So I guess we did kind of get along. Just lucky, I guess."

This is the most talkative Grandma's been. Not just on our trip, but maybe ever. I'm not certain what's putting her in this mood; it's not just the wine. I definitely want to encourage it. Something about the trip, or Kingston, has greased her wheels of recollection. "What else happened?"

"It's so long ago now, but I remember there was a lot to learn. In my second year I failed a big exam. I couldn't believe it. Again some of the girls thought I was in for it. I ended up getting called down to see the nursing superintendent."

"What happened?"

"The problem was I hadn't bothered to memorize everything. That's what we were supposed to do, memorize the material. I didn't see the point in that."

"But you understood it?"

"Oh, sure, I knew it like the back of my hand, but just not in the same exact phrasing we were taught. I knew it, all right. I just said it in my own words."

"And what did they do?"

"I guess they let me redo the exam. I decided I'd better toe the line and do it the way they wanted. So I memorized it."

Her eyes are lighting up, twinkling again. My mind is eared to her words.

"In our third year, our last year, we worked six days a week. And on the seventh we still worked, but just a half-day. Remember, this was still before the war; good thing I was young."

"Craziness," I say. "I feel like there's so much talk about how we work too much now, how work has taken over our lives. But I don't think any school or college could get away with working their students six and a half days a week."

"I'm not sure. Maybe the difference now is not being able to leave work. When we stopped working, we stopped. We did other things. We weren't always connected to it the way it seems people are now with their computers and phones. I'm not sure."

Our supper arrives. I can smell the fresh basil. The cheese on the pizza is bubbling around the edges when they lay it down at our table. The server sets the orange fries beside the pizza. They're in a lattice-style basket. There's a spicy dipping sauce that comes with them.

"I've talked your ear off again," says Grandma, placing her napkin over her lap. "It must be all this good food. I never talk like this at home."

"It's interesting, Grandma."

"Well, you must be starving. Dig in," she says.

"You first," I reply.

"No, no, you go first."

I take her plate and give her a slice and some fries.

"Why am I talking so much?" she says again, more to herself, ignoring the food. "It really is silly. You don't need to hear all this."

"It's not at all. We've known each other my entire life, but there's a lot we don't know about each other."

"I'm not used to talking like this, I guess," she says. "I just don't want to bore you."

"I'm not either, Grandma. And you don't have to worry about that."

Grandma slowly brings her glass up, asking for a cheers. I clink hers with mine. "Here's to stories," she says. "Old and new."

"And memories," I say.

She holds up her glass a moment longer as I take my sip. "Yes," she says, "and to not letting them go to waste."

9:18 p.m.

THE RAIN IS still falling when we (Grandma) pay the bill and head back out to the car. This time we don't jog. I go first and pull my car up as close to the door as I can. I watch her hold her jacket together at the neck, bow her head, and step carefully around the puddles. Her limp is worse. "Your car's sounding a little loud tonight. Is it running okay?"

"Yup, I think so. It's always pretty loud."

I pull out onto the road. There's very little traffic in Kingston at this time. The headlights of the few cars we pass reflect up off the wet asphalt.

"Did you see the woman eating alone in the restaurant?" Grandma asks about five minutes into our drive.

"Which one?" I ask.

But I know who she's talking about. I saw her. She was an elderly lady in brown cords, a black sweater, and glasses.

She was drinking coffee from a white mug and eating a sandwich on whole wheat bread; a grilled cheese, I think. Her hands were thin and heavily wrinkled. She had short hair under her beret-style cap. Her jacket had been set un-neatly on the back of her chair. She appeared quite content eating her supper alone. So it's strange I found the scene agonizing.

"She was the one a few tables over to our right," says Grandma. "She was eating a sandwich, I think."

She obviously made an impression on Grandma as well. "Yeah, I do remember her. Kinda sad, I thought, she had to eat alone."

Alone is my default meal position. It's been strange to

share meals with another human this week. So it's not just the woman's aloneness that I found gloomy. Something else, I'm not sure what.

Grandma turns toward me. "I didn't think she seemed sad. Not at all. I thought how nice it was that she was treating herself to dinner at a restaurant. She must not have felt like cooking tonight."

"But I wonder if she's alone." I meant to say, *I wonder if she's lonely.*

"Maybe," says Grandma. "I would like to think she might be alone and that she likes it."

I exhale to respond. I think I know what Grandma means. I think I do.

"When I go to the mall," she says, "to pay bills at the bank or get my hair done, sometimes I walk down to the other end. And I'll be alone. There's a Bulk Barn there where I can get honey-coated cashews and smoky almonds. There's also a little restaurant. Sometimes I'll just go in and sit down and treat myself. Just for a coffee, or breakfast if I'm hungry. Nothing fancy. I ask for one sausage and some scrambled eggs."

"That sounds nice."

"It is."

We pull into the driveway. We don't dawdle outside tonight like we did last night. The rain is too heavy, and again Grandma's hopeful we can catch the end of the hockey game. Her Ottawa Senators are playing, the second night of a back-to-back. I make us some fennel and ginger tea, which I can't believe I have, as she settles in front of the game.

While I'm waiting for the kettle to boil, she calls out that Ottawa is losing 3–0. By the time I get to the TV with our beverage, it's 3–1. Grandma is sitting on the couch with a pillow behind her back and one at her side.

As we watch the game, sipping our tea, I'm still thinking about that woman in the restaurant and thinking about Grandma eating her one-sausage breakfast alone in the mall restaurant.

With Ottawa scoring another goal, making the score 3–2, Grandma has perked up again. "I guess all that talking at supper has put me in a reminiscent mood . . . I'm sorry."

"No, it's great, Grandma. It's interesting to hear this stuff. I didn't know any of it."

"Are you sure?"

"Of course."

"Well, I hate to even bring this up, it's really quite silly of me, but I put a few old pictures into my grip before you picked me up. Would you like to see them?" I intuit that she almost didn't ask. It required great effort on her part.

"I would love to."

She retreats to her room. I sit alone with the muted commercials. I'm looking at them but not watching them closely. The images seem to move even faster, seem more absurd and circusy, more pompous and visually irritating, without sound. Down the hall I hear rummaging.

When Grandma returns, she's wearing her reading glasses and humming under her breath. She has a stack of photos in her hand. They aren't in a book or envelope. They're just loose in her hand. She sits beside me on the couch. We both sit stooped under the single lamp.

"Here," she says, passing me the first one. "This one's of your grandpa and me. We were still living in the apartment then."

The photo is smaller than I'm used to seeing. The paper is thicker. It has a white border along the edges. Grandma and Grandpa look to be my age now. The picture is taken outside, beside a tree. Grandma is rake-thin. She's wearing a long dress that hangs just above her ankles. Grandpa's in a suit and tie and hat. He has his right arm around her shoulders.

The next few she hands me are also of her and Grandpa. Several show them on a winter's day, pulling a sled with their kids, my mom included.

"Okay, there's this one, too, and don't worry, it's the last." Grandma turns away as she hands me the picture. She's re-engaged in the hockey. Ottawa has been pressing, and it looks like they just might complete the comeback. "Now, how's the game going, how are we doing?" she asks the TV.

I look down at the photo. It shows a young woman, maybe in her early to mid-twenties. She's in what I assume is a full nursing uniform of the time and is seated at a plain wooden desk. Behind her is a stack of files on a shelf and a bulletin board mounted on the wall. She has a pencil in her right hand, and whoever took the picture has interrupted her solitude, disrupted whatever she's writing. Maybe a diary entry, or study notes. Maybe she's writing a letter.

It's difficult to decipher the lighting in the room. I think it looks dark. I imagine it was taken at night. Somehow it feels late. She looks like she'd prefer not to have her picture taken, like it's an inconvenience. If there were a thought bubble above her head it would read, "Hurry up."

The nurse is smiling blithely, though, until the photographer leaves her be. Then she can return to her work.

THURSDAY

8:43 a.m.

I'M ONLY JUST inferring. She's trying to tell me she's waiting without actually telling me. Instead of calling through the door, or even knocking, Grandma's been coughing, tepidly, for about three minutes, off and on. She doesn't want to pester me. I've realized this the past three days. Grandma's preferred presence as a guest is to blend into the walls. She's ready for the bathroom, but only when it's free.

I've been in here for a while. I splash a fifth or sixth handful of warm water over my face and wipe my hands on my shirt (which dampens the front of my shirt but doesn't fully dry my hands).

Outside the door, waiting with Grandma, is another day. Like a small plastic object you find at the back of your kitchen junk drawer, it should be used for something, but I can't decide what. I also know I can't just ignore or discard it, like I could if alone.

"Is that you, Grandma?"

"Ohhh." She sounds surprised. "Good morning, dear. Yup, it's only me."

"Good morning. I'll be out in a second." I plant my face in the small green towel hanging beside the sink for a proper dry.

"Not to worry, there's no rush."

I open the door. Grandma's standing arms akimbo, dressed in a red sweater, black pants, and her dark blue Hush Puppies shoes. Her smartly assembled outfit can't hide her unwell complexion. She's elegant, but more indisposed than yesterday. She looks smaller, shorter. Her nose is as red as her sweater.

"How are you feeling today? How's the cold?"

She sniffs through deeply congested nostrils before waving my question away. "Better, I think. I'm on the mend, that's for sure."

"Really, are you sure? Did you sleep okay?"

"Yes, you don't have to ask me. I always do. And anyway, I'm certainly much better than yesterday. I'll be completely back to normal by tomorrow."

Yesterday she said she was fine, that it sounded much worse than it was. This morning she's telling me she's much better than yesterday. She sounds worse. I'm flummoxed by her staunch stoicism.

"I'm glad you're wearing your warm sweater today. It looks colder outside. It's a nice colour. The red suits you." Only for shirts, not chapped noses.

"You think? I usually prefer blue."

"Yeah, it looks great." And it does, but this is also adding to the pressure of coming up with exciting and interesting things to do today. If Grandma was greeting me each morning in her nightgown and housecoat, with hair askew, we'd be equals. I'd at least be able to suggest we stick closer to my typical routine of staying in my apartment.

"Have you looked outside yet? I was just looking out the

window." She taps my shoulder on her way into the bathroom. "It's not raining."

I leave Grandma to her ablutions. I find the kitchen as I left it. I recognize the crumbs from my late-night peanut butter sandwich. How can we break our fast this morning? Something other than toast and condiment would be nice.

I stand in front of the open fridge, scratching the back of my thigh. I fling cupboards open and then closed. It seems like I spend the bulk of my money on food. And yet, I never have anything to eat. Ever.

I move back to the fridge again. It's identical to the way it was the first time. I never omit this immediate follow-up fridge examination, as if in the time it takes to open and close the cereal cupboard, that jar of expired gherkins will be replaced by a fresh strawberry Danish dusted with icing sugar. I have no conscious memory of purchasing these inedible gherkins. I can't recall a time in my life ever enjoying (or even consuming) a gherkin. I honestly don't know what a gherkin is. Yet there they are, winking at me from their lot between the mayo and mint jelly.

I shut the fridge. Toast and cheese isn't the end of the world, I suppose.

The toaster's elements are glowing orange and the slices are somewhere between bread and toast when Grandma joins me in the kitchen. The kitchen fills with the unappetizing scent of burntness. Crumbs or an old crust must be stuck at the bottom. "Good morning, again," I say.

"Well, good morning, again."

She steps past me to the window. I'm not sure what she's looking at but she's doing it purposefully. I set our plates and knives on the table. She stays by the window, peering outside. She's looking for something. When the toast pops, Grandma turns. "I thought I could smell toast. I hoped I could. I do love my toast."

"That's good." Because that's all I ever give you. "We both love our toast."

I set the coffee to brew before carrying a tray of toast to the table, where Grandma has seated herself in her usual chair. "I can't believe I'm hungry again after our great supper last night. But I am."

"Me too," I say.

I unlid the butter dish and set the cheese plate beside Grandma. "What else do you need, Grandma? Would you like some jam . . . maybe some gherkins or something?"

"No, this looks wonderful. I'm fine."

We're dressing our toast when she pauses in mid-spread and looks up from her plate. "Did you have any funny dreams last night?"

"No, not really. None that I can remember. Did you?" I take my first bite.

"I think I did. But I can't remember, either. I can never remember the dreams I want to. But I think it had something to do with when I started nursing, or it took place around that time or something."

Grandma finishes her prep while I force myself to slow down my eating by taking smaller bites and actually chewing.

"So, do you remember why you got into nursing in the first place?"

"You mean in my dream?"

"No, I'm curious about why you did it in real life."

"When I got into nursing initially, it was because I wanted to be a psych nurse. But it didn't work out like that."

"How come?"

"Well, I was picked with another nurse in my class to be in the operating room. That sort of changed everything."

"Psych nurse to the operating room? That's a significant shift. Were you happy to do it?"

"It was very different. But it was an opportunity, so I took it." She pauses to spread melting butter across her toast. "I liked it. I enjoyed being part of the surgeries. It was thrilling. After graduating, I was hired to the staff at Winnipeg General. I loved my job."

"So how did you end up at working at the barracks?"

"It's funny, it was so long ago, but I can clearly remember the day. I'd been working a long shift. It had been busy. Near the end, one of the surgeons came by and asked the supervising nurse if she would consider joining Fort Osborne Barracks. I was cleaning up, putting some instruments away, and could hear the conversation. She was telling him how she didn't want to. She had too many things going on. She was engaged to be married. She was planning on having a family. That was her priority, I guess."

I finish my first piece and lean back in my chair. Grandma's toast is fully buttered and waiting. She's yet to take a bite.

"And then she turns to me and says, 'But she wants to join.' The surgeon walked over and asked me if that was true. I told him, yes, I'd had my name in to join since before I'd graduated. I knew him from working at the hospital, and we always got on, so when he heard I was interested, he put my name forward. It wasn't long at all before I'd been accepted into the barracks and the army."

"Did you know you wanted to be in the army?"

"Well, I wouldn't say I'd thought a lot about it, to tell you the truth. But, yes, by that time, it just seemed like the thing to do. Iain, it was an adventure to me. I was young, I wanted to travel, and let's be honest, times were different back then. The world was very different. We knew what was happening in Europe. We knew it wasn't good. So of course I was going to do it."

"Let me get us some coffee," I say, retrieving the pot and two mugs.

"Thanks, dear. I'd love one." She picks up her toast but continues with her story. "My dad had joined the army during the First World War, the same year he arrived in Canada. It was the Canadian Army he joined, too, even though he'd just arrived. I figured I'd do the same. Why wouldn't I? The other thing was the pay. Nurses were very underpaid in those days. I wasn't going to be making much money. But in the army, nurses were automatically given the rank of officer. This meant a significant increase in pay compared to just staying on at the hospital. So, I guess there were lots of reasons why it happened the way it did."

She accepts her mug and takes a sip, nodding her approval.

"And it also had to do with Donald, the one I used to shoot pucks at."

She offers a look that I'm not sure I've seen before, a coy earnestness.

"Donald joined up with the air force. He'd obviously never flown a plane before. The only training they gave him was a pamphlet to read. Imagine that: flying a plane, in a war, after reading an instructional pamphlet."

"If it all happened today, I bet you would have been a doctor, though." This doesn't come out the way I wanted. I mean it as a compliment but it sounds more like a slight.

"I liked being a nurse. That's what I wanted to be."

"But the military part. And the war that was going on. And going overseas in a ship. And all that. You didn't even know *where* you were going. Weren't you worried about that? You must have been scared."

Grandma now refocuses on me directly. I've taken history courses and have read many books about many different wars. I've studied strategy, battlefields, and the philosophy of war. But how frightening is it to be in one? We've been nibbling our toast and sipping our coffee as we chat. She sets down her coffee now. Her expression changes to a veneer of unobscured implacability.

It's another look I'm unfamiliar with, a look that affects me physically. I feel myself sitting up in my chair. Her eyes no longer show her usual cordiality but a toughness bordering on malice. "Iain, I was never scared. Not once."

I don't think I would have been able to say the same, but I believe her completely.

"I was never worried about anything I did or was involved in. I just never really worried too much." Again she pauses. "But I was always concerned for Donald. I often thought about him. I just hoped if something were to happen, it would be to me, but not to him, not Donald. He was my little brother, after all, and he was so young."

She never would have brought this up on her own. The fact that she sailed across the ocean into a war and was never scared. It's a vital piece of information for me to learn about her. I never knew it until now. It never came up. I never asked.

"Huh" and "yeah" is what I offer in return. There's obviously more I'd like to say. Maybe if I think about it for a while I'll be able to tell her how impressed I am. It's not really about being impressed, though. That seems to grossly simplify what I feel. We turn back to our breakfast and eat in silence.

It's Rufus who takes our attention from the food. Rufus is what she must have been looking for this morning before she sat down. He's at the door, looking in. Rufus, my neighbour's cat.

"I just had a feeling he'd come by this morning. I saw him outside last night, when I was up to use the bathroom," she says.

Rufus is a big black feline with whiskers that branch out from his snout like pipe cleaners. If Grandma saw him, he was likely outside all night. He's wet and desperately wants in.

I feel bad, sure, but am also reluctant. He's not only big but aggressive. He tends to nip. He's not my cat, and it is very tricky to get him back out once he's in. He makes me feel uneasy in the same way a rabid muskrat would.

"We should let him in for a bit, right?" says Grandma, standing up. "How can we resist those eyes looking in?"

"Well..."

It's easy to resist — just shift ninety degrees in your seat and turn your back to the door.

Grandma starts touching the glass where Rufus is sniffing, as if she's visiting him in cat prison. Which is where he should be. It's then I remember, for the first time the entire trip, that Grandma has a cat of her own. She adopted Pippa early this year. I haven't asked about Pippa at all. "Grandma, I totally forgot. Are you missing Pippa since you've been away?"

"I guess I am. Sure. She'll be fine, though. Have I told you what she's been doing to me lately?"

"No."

Grandma can't restrain her smile now that she's talking about her own cat. "She makes me take a nap every afternoon. Sometime after lunch she'll start swirling around my feet until I go and lie down on the couch with my blanket. Then she climbs up on top of me and we both fall asleep. I've never been much of a napper" — she laughs — "but then again, I've never been a cat person, either. I always liked animals but never thought I'd have a cat."

I'm staring at Rufus. Those whiskers are way too long. He lost his tail a few years back, after an accident. I think he was hit by a car. It's all very sad, but he carries on untroubled. I think it's affected me more. The lack of tail, that furry yet bare rump, continues to unsettle me. I wouldn't be able to nod off if he was in the same room, let alone lying across my chest.

"When we wake up from our nap, we always have a little chat. Lately, I've been asking Pippa who's older, me or her. She's getting a little grey beard. I still think I might have her beat. But just barely. She's around eighteen or nineteen, which must be around ninety-two in human years. I think we're both surprised we're still around. Neither has many naps left in us, I don't think."

I turn away from Rufus. "Are you surprised, Grandma? I mean, living so long." It's something I've been meaning to ask her for a while.

"I'm amazed, Iain. No one in my family has ever lived this long, not even close. It doesn't make a lot of sense to me. I never ever would have guessed I'd be around into my *nineties*. No way."

"So, do you think a lot about dying, then?"

"You know, I don't. At least not with any despair. I'm not scared of dying. And here's the thing: it will happen when it happens. Did you ever hear of the time I woke up beside the land mine?"

"No."

"It was in Sicily. A fellow I knew had a Jeep and offered to take me for a ride. We ended up going farther than we should have. We lost track of time. It got dark and we were still out. So we decided we'd better stop for the night, sleep on the side of the road, and go back first thing in the morning."

"And did you?"

"We did. We slept outside. But at dawn I woke to him grabbing my arm. He was very serious and talking slowly. He was telling me not to move. He helped me up. For the entire night I'd been asleep right near a mine. We hadn't seen it in the dark."

She swivels from the door and bends down to the bottom drawer, where I keep the flour, sugar, and oatmeal. She opens it and takes something out, something I didn't know was in there. She must have brought the bag of cat treats from home. I must have mentioned Rufus to Grandma.

"You know, I always thought George would live longer than me. We both did. He never would have believed I'd last this long," she says. "So what do you think, should we let him in?"

She doesn't wait for an answer but opens the door a crack. Rufus sniffs his way in and curls around her feet. She scratches his back along his spine. "What a good boy... you're such a good boy," she says.

"Watch out he doesn't bite you," I say, taking a step back behind Grandma. "Sometimes, you know, he bites."

"No, no, he won't, he's fine. I brought something with me in case I saw him." She shakes a pile of the tiny brown pellets onto the floor. Grandma watches in undiluted satisfaction as Rufus scarfs up the salmon-flavoured morsels like he needs them to live.

12:38 p.m.

"WELL, LOOKS LIKE we'll need to kill some time. Sorry."

"Oh, that's okay. How much time do we need to kill?"

"About an hour and a half," I grumble.

"Okay, an hour and a half."

We're sitting in my idling car. I'm watching the exhaust fumes billowing up from behind in the rear-view mirror. We're at the entrance to the ferry. The one working windshield wiper in its tauntingly *nah-nah-nah-boo-boo* way is waving back and forth at me on top speed. I've had my greatest moment of inspiration in the past four days. I decided I'd take Grandma over to Wolfe Island.

Wolfe Island is a mostly rural island in Lake Ontario. It's just south of Kingston, at the mouth of the St. Lawrence River. It's a summer destination, for cottagers mostly, as only around a couple of thousand people call the island home year round. It reminds me of Toronto Island, how when you get on it you feel like you're a long way away from the city you left.

We'd been sitting around after breakfast, sipping second cups of coffee while I read over glossy pamphlets I'd snagged from the tourist office. Each pamphlet was for a different museum.

"Here, what do you think about the marine museum? It looks kinda cool. Or the woodworking museum?" Each of my offers was met by an unreliable "Sure, we could do that."

That's when I had my idea.

I told her my plan about going to Wolfe Island and was waiting for balloons to drop from the ceiling when Grandma asked what time the ferry left: On the half-hour, I told her. We had eighteen minutes.

The ferry leaves every hour. And it is on the half-hour. But that's in the morning. It shifts to on the hour after lunch. We missed the last ferry by five minutes. We could see it pulling away. The sky was just starting to sprinkle when we jogged out to my car. It's raining harder now.

"Do you want to go back home?"

"Seems a shame when we're already out."

We're only ten minutes from home. There are limited

options for things to do in Kingston on a weekday morning.

"Yeah, I guess so." We could always go back to the café.

She brings her hands together on her lap. I sense Grandma has her own idea. "Is there a liquor store nearby?"

"Pardon?"

"Just curious if there's a liquor store. We could kill some time there."

The thought hadn't occurred to me. It's not a terrible idea. "Actually, there is. Just about a block away."

"Let's go," she says, definitively.

OUR DOWNTOWN LIQUOR store is a one- or two-minute drive from the ferry terminal. I'm usually there with expediency as my aim, to run in and out, to grab a bottle of wine or a six-pack of beer. It's a large store, with lots of varieties of wines and spirits. I've never just wandered around inside before. The store has never been a means to me. Just an end. But Grandma and I have time to kill.

Usually the few parking spots come at a premium. At peak hours, between 4 and 6 p.m., it's unheard of to land a spot. At this time of day, when alcohol is rarely a priority, there are no cars at all. The grocery store lot across the street isn't even half full. Grandma chats as we walk in under the umbrella. We are getting used to the small space underneath the ripped nylon.

"The last time I was in the liquor store back home, I was very embarrassed," she's saying. "I took a young guy aside and asked for a bottle of Crest sherry. He couldn't find it. I was adamant. I said I knew they had some because I'd bought it there before. So he had to go and get their ordering sheet and bring it out, and we tried to find Crest sherry, which is my favourite. Anyway, it finally dawned on me. Crest is my damn toothpaste. The sherry is Croft."

We're just inside when Grandma finishes her toothpaste story. She's winded from the stroll, and giggly. The store's only just opened. Customers are clearly unexpected. Apart from the two employees on shift, we're alone with all the glass and booze.

One worker is standing at a cash register. The other is handling a mop in the sparkling-wine aisle. He stops his mopping as we stroll by. He nods hello, but his expression is one of surprise. Yet again, seeing an old, small, white-haired lady accompanied by a (much) younger, bespectacled, bearded guy has surprised an onlooker.

Liquor stores like this are built to accommodate large crowds. They aren't meant for two people. We both know we aren't searching for anything specifically. Neither of us knows much about wine.

We start our ramble in Australia. I tell Grandma I've tried the Little Penguin Merlot before. That's the only one I've sampled. Next is New Zealand. We make our way over to France, and then Italy. I point out the Pinots like they're somehow significant. We stop at any oddly shaped bottles. We point out the whimsical or gimmicky names to each other. "Sibling Rivalry," says Grandma. "Have you ever tried that?"

I shake my head. "Only the real thing." She doesn't hear me and continues along. She half hums, half whistles, faintly.

With her a few steps ahead, I can discern she's still favouring her left leg. This is the first time I've had this perspective, a couple of steps behind. I thought maybe she'd been limping worse this morning, but haven't been able to confirm it until now. She never lets on if asked directly. It must be that sore knee still bothering her. The one from her fall.

Our voyage continues along the wall of whisky, a soft spot for Grandma. Scotch of all varieties, blends and single malts, acknowledges us from the shelves as we pass.

"Maybe we should get a small bottle, Grandma. You still like the odd pinch of single malt, don't you?"

"Oh, well, sure. Grab one. I was just thinking, I can still remember the first time I ever had a drink. It was a week or so before Christmas. I'd been out babysitting for a neighbour.

"When the parents got home from their party, they'd been drinking and were feeling good and offered me a glass of wine. My mother wasn't a drinker at all, so when I got home, I remember rushing in and going right up to her and just breathing in her face. She could smell it on me, all right."

With the store empty like this, it's like we're in a museum of sorts. Not one advertised in any of my pamphlets, but a museum of our own reflections. Each bottle is holding a liquid memory. At least for Grandma.

"I can't remember my first drink," I tell her. "I don't think it would make much of a story, anyway." I have a cloudy image of shotgunning a warm king can of Milwaukee's Best behind the sheep barn at my parents' farm.

We continue along to the clear spirits. "Now you should get something for yourself. You like gin, don't you? I'm buying, my treat."

"I thought I was buying."

"No, no, dear. Let me treat you."

"I feel like you've been doing all the treating." I'm unequivocally certain she has.

"No, I want to get this," she says. I oblige and pick a small bottle of gin to go along with our Scotch. "And what about a nice bottle of wine for supper?"

"What do you feel like?" I ask.

"Whatever *you* want, dear."

I jog back to the nearest region, France. I haven't had Beaujolais in a long time. I should have grabbed a basket when we came in. I didn't know we'd be buying so much. When I get back to Grandma, she's distracted by another bottle. It takes her a few seconds to intuit my presence.

"I can't believe this," she says without looking up. "I haven't seen this in years and years." She holds up a plastic mickey of Southern Comfort.

"Huh, I don't think I've ever had that."

"It was one of the first drinks I had with George. Neither of us had tried it before. We hadn't known each other very long, only a few weeks, and we decided, I can't remember why, but we decided to take a little trip for the weekend. You see, we were *always* doing that. So we went down to the States. I can also remember how his sisters really didn't approve."

"Oh?"

"Well, we didn't know each other very well yet, or for very long, and of course we weren't married. That was a no-no."

"But you went anyway?"

"Of course. We'd decided to go away and we did. Anyway, that's what they served us, wherever we were, I can't remember. We even bought a bottle when we got home. Although we never really drank it. It was more for the memory."

"Do you guys need a hand finding anything?" It's the guy with the mop.

"Actually, I think we're fine, man. Just on our way to the cash," I answer. Grandma smiles at him. He carries his filthy mop back to his bucket of water.

Walking to the car, I stop. "Here, take the keys and I'll meet you in the car. I'll be right back."

I almost slip when I catch my foot on the curb, jogging back into the store.

1:38 p.m.

THE SKIES HAVE opened.

It's raining harder now than it has at any other point of the trip. It's raining harder now than at any time in my life, or human history. Not drops but beefy, biblical sheets of water are falling on the windshield.

Without the wipers (even the one that's not broken), visibility would be nil. There are two cars in front of us. Four behind us. To our left is the high grey metal side of the ferry boat. To our right is another car, actually a truck that is at least two or three feet higher than my low-riding Toyota. Even without the wind and rain our visibility would be nil. We are sardined into place.

"It's so fun to be on a ferry," Grandma's insisting, "out on the water like this. It's just so fun." Irony and sarcasm don't suit Grandma, so I'm taking her comment at face value.

"Yeah, well, it's not really what I pictured when I had the idea. I was kinda hoping we could actually see things."

"Like what?"

"Oh, I don't know, the lake for one."

"It's still fun," she says.

I brought some more tapes out to the car with me this morning. I slide one in the deck: a homemade Woody Guthrie mix. Twenty or so seconds in, I switch it off abruptly, turning toward Grandma. "We could go up to the observation deck. We'd need the umbrella, but at least..." As I'm suggesting it, I catch the absurdity. Neither of us wants to be out in this storm. And that's what it is — it's a full-blown spring storm.

Grandma has started her tuneless humming again. I'm watching an elderly fellow exit the indoor seating area. He looks around and walks out into the rain. He moves past a few cars, walking purposefully down the middle aisle. He's not dressed to be out in the rain.

He shuffles between the two cars in front of us, squeezing by the side mirrors. He's standing right outside Grandma's door now. He's drenched. There's a firm tap on her window. She looks at me as if to say, *What the hell?* I shrug my shoulders. She lowers her window. Instantly her forearm is soaked.

The man doesn't waste any time, gripping the half-opened window and bringing his face into the car. His bushy white brows look like carports for his eyes. Grandma leans away from the window, from him. He's staring directly at her when he poses his question. "Have you seen the Amish girls?"

Grandma stares back. She swivels her head to me. I answer for her. "Sorry, what's that?"

"Have you seen the Amish girls?" This time he sounds more aggravated than curious. Again Grandma and I look at each other. I know we're both thinking the same thing. Who, pray tell, are the fucking *Amish* girls? Is this some musical theatre performance on Wolfe Island? Maybe he's trying to sell tickets — a Gilbert and Sullivan I'm unfamiliar with?

"I'm not sure," says Grandma.

He's getting more flustered and wet. He seems angered by our lack of concrete response. He's ignoring the rivulets of water flowing freely down his wrinkled face.

"Sorry, but no, we haven't seen the Amish girls."

He shakes his head in disgust, releases his grip on the door ledge, and is gone. He waddles back to his shelter without stopping at any other cars.

"What was that?" asks Grandma, when the window is back up.

"I have no idea, very weird. I think he was asking about, uh, Amish girls."

Grandma just smiles. "I told you it was going to be a fun ride."

Ten minutes later, we've docked. We're waiting for our turn to accelerate off the boat. Our row is last. It's Grandma who sees them. She taps my arm and points to the top of the ship. There are four girls distinctly dressed in Amish attire.

They are wet and look doleful.

"Well, those are the Amish girls," says Grandma. "But I don't know what happened to our friend."

I see the man in the car to our right for the first time as he moves past. He's wearing armless sunglasses, like Morpheus in *The Matrix*. He grins at me and points at my broken licence plate. There have been no Daliesque melting clocks. Regardless, this has been a surreal boat ride.

Surreal, weird, wet. Hardly fun.

JUST LIKE AT the liquor store, we've found ourselves in another empty lot. Mine is the only car here. The painted yellow lines marking each allotted space are faded from weather, I imagine, not use. I pull into the spot right in the middle, facing the water. Lake Ontario lies calmly in front of us.

"I can't believe the rain has let up; it's almost stopped. It was so heavy before. And it almost seems like the clouds are clearing, too. You can see so much farther out to the lake now. We might even get some sun."

"That would be something," I say, stepping out of the car, stretching.

We've decided to get some lunch before we explore further. We leave the car and walk across the street to a restaurant.

I packed some sandwiches, but something went wrong. I'd put the peanut-butter-and-jellies in my bag, but when I retrieved my water bottle from the bag on the ferry, I caught a whiff of something horrid. Once inside the bag, the sammies took on an entirely new smell. Outside of the bag they were fine, but after the bag smell, I was done. I told Grandma we'd better just have lunch at a restaurant.

We enter one large, open space with wooden tables and wooden booths along the windows. There's a hardwood dance floor and a large bar in the corner to our left. It, too, is made of wood.

None of the tables is occupied. Seated at the bar are three men wearing sweat-stained ball caps. They're drinking coffee (presumably) and don't seem to be talking much. Or moving. Or breathing. Every so often, one of them brings his cup to his mouth and may or may not sip. Like everything else, they also might be made of wood, except their hands, which look like uneven balls of clay. They aren't holding their mugs with human appendages but with gnarled fingerling potatoes.

We wipe our wet feet on the frayed blue mat. Before we reach our table, Grandma informs me she's in the mood for soup. I confirm I could also consume some hot soup. The bartender arrives with menus and tells us he'll also be our waiter.

"It smells so good in here," says Grandma.

"Do you guys have any soup?"

"Yup, still a couple bowls left. It's cream of asparagus. It's delicious. That was my lunch, too."

Grandma insists I get something else. Soup won't be enough for me. I tell her a dense cream soup with bread and butter probably will be. Her eyebrow shoots skyward. I ask for the menus back.

We each decide on an order of fish and chips. "Homemade beer batter," he tells us, "really delicious. I had some earlier."

I come close to ordering a club sandwich (that I won't eat) just to see if he tells me it's delicious and that he also had it for lunch.

It doesn't take long for the soup and fish to arrive at our table. The soup is steaming and the fish is golden brown and glistening with that inviting blush of grease.

A few spoonfuls into our soup and bites into our fish, he's back at the table. He's just topped up the farmers' cups. He's holding the coffee pot casually at his side like a top hat. "So, where are you guys from?"

Everyone always seems to know we're on vacation. Sometimes they want to chat. This is rare when I'm out somewhere eating alone. Usually I'm just left to consume in private. I wipe some tartar sauce off the corner of my lip. "Ottawa," I say. "Well, I live in Kingston now. But she's from Ottawa." Grandma points to my nose and makes a wiping motion. I wipe my nose, too.

"What are you guys doing on the island?"

"We're on vacation," says Grandma, setting down her cutlery. She picks up her napkin off her lap and wipes the corners of her mouth daintily.

"Cool. I grew up on a farm near Ottawa. But now I'm trying to make a go of it around here. It's a nice area. I'm loving it." He talks quickly.

"Have you been on the island long?" wonders Grandma. Grandma's genuinely engaged; she's interested. Whereas I'm just impostering someone who isn't more concerned for his cooling soup and haddock.

"Only two weeks. And I like it." He lowers his voice. "But it takes a while to get to know the locals." He motions toward the farmers. "It's nice to be working here, near a kitchen. I'd like to work as a chef one day."

"That's wonderful. Iain here also loves to cook. He could be a chef one day, too. He's been making me some amazing meals."

"Well," I say, "I mean, I'm not sure..." I don't think there's a booming demand for a toast-and-cheese-only restaurant.

He sets the pot down on our table and pulls up a neighbouring chair to my right. "Do you ever watch the Food Network?"

"Oh, we were talking about that. Iain loves the Food Network. You're always watching it, aren't you?"

"Well, I mean, sometimes I might..."

"Really, eh? Yeah, I love it, too."

"I always want to watch the hockey," Grandma's admitting, "but I get the feeling Iain would rather be on the food channel."

"Ha, I'm like that, too. Amazing! I'll take Bobby Flay over Sid Crosby any day."

Have you ever watched tartar sauce congeal? I don't mean see it *once* it's reached room temperature. I mean actively observe it *as* it warms. I don't recommend it. It's a wretched evolution. It not only congeals but changes colour. It starts out chilly, white, and appetizing when it arrives fresh from the fridge. Then it becomes yellowish, sluggish, as you leave it be.

"So is this a quiet day for you guys?" asks Grandma.

"It's been like this most days since I've been here. I guess last year there was a real boom on the island. Our restaurants were filled pretty much every day. It was because they were building the turbines."

"We can see those wind turbines from Kingston," I say. "I wondered when those went up."

"The island was full of contractors and builders. They had to eat. It was great for business but I think tough on the residents, who are used to the normal pace of island life. For the most part that's what they like around here. Can't blame them, really."

"Are there a lot of people who live on the island?" asks Grandma.

"Not really, a couple thousand, maybe. Obviously more in the summer. It's not a huge place, I think only about thirty kilometres long."

Ten minutes later, we've moved from island politics to covering the many uses of chicken stock (homemade, of course). Now we're touching on the nature of infidelity. I didn't anticipate this last topic. I have to admit, he's winning me over. He's poured each of us (including himself) a coffee. "I've had the same girl for over a year now. I'd never, ever cheat on her. How could you ever live with yourself?"

"It's true," I say. Somehow I've been promoted to CEO of the discussion. It's not a title I covet. Grandma held the position for about three minutes when she got the ball rolling. But now she's balancing a piece of fish on her fork with a few strands of creamy coleslaw.

"It's not worth it. And it's lying. It means you're a liar." I'm just waiting for him to reach out and help himself to a chip on my plate. He's been eyeing them longingly.

"You're right," I say. "I agree."

After he returns to his post behind the bar, I think about eating more but cover the remainder of my meal with my napkin. I push my plate away. I watch Grandma eat every last morsel of edible fare on her plate.

"So," she says loud enough for everyone in the restaurant, including him, to hear, "what was he saying?"

"He doesn't like people who cheat on their girlfriends," I whisper. "And also that chicken stock is best with some fresh thyme."

"I could tell he was a good guy. Now, what are you going to get for dessert? And remember, it's my treat."

IT WAS MY suggestion to drive west, along what I believe is the island's main road. It was the faithful bartender/waiter who told me we could get a good look at those turbines if we went this way. A leisurely drive through the island farmland seems about right after our heavy lunch, even if we don't find the turbines.

The island is very green. I consider it a visual substitute for our lack of salad at lunch. Grandma is commenting on how quiet and peaceful it is. She says it reminds her of the area around Lilac Hill, my parents' farm.

Ten minutes or so down the road, we come to a gravel lane on our left. "Should we try going down there? What do you think? Or do you want to go back?"

"I think we should try it."

I turn and accelerate excessively, spitting gravel out behind us. We haven't passed any other cars, or people. The gravel road enhances the mood of isolation that comes with being on an island.

We've seen a few of the wind turbines already on our drive. We've been pointing them out to one another. "There's one," Grandma would say as we passed, or "Another windmill to your left." But now, unfolding in front of us, is an entire field of them. Not four or five but twenty, thirty, maybe forty. They're like giant creatures grazing on the wind.

I slow our pace and pull off the road, up to the entrance. This is the wind farm. I've read a few articles about it. It was big news for a while in Kingston. There's been a great debate regarding the turbines and if they are a positive or negative thing for the island.

It's entirely different to see them so close, so many together. From Kingston they look like lawn ornaments, modern and pretty but not serving a purpose. When you're here beside them, their labour is clear. I can also understand why those living near the turbines would find them invasive.

"They are graceful," says Grandma.

"They are. But there've been some complaints from people who live around here. People in other countries say living close to wind turbines has made them sick."

There are no electrical cables running from the mills. It gives them each an air of individuality. Each is rooted directly into the earth.

"There must be some lines buried underground."

"You think?"

"Must be," she says. "That's the point after all, to generate power."

"I wonder if they make a loud noise. You'd think they would, but looking at them this close, they look so sleek. It's strange, but they almost look noiseless."

I turn off the engine and step out of the car. Grandma stays in her seat. I walk around and lean on the hood above the right tire. Grandma's window is down.

"I think I can hear them now," I say.

"Yes, but it's not nearly as loud as you'd think."

"No. There's a noise, but it's subtle."

"It sounds like strong wind. How many are there in total?"

I wish I knew more. I should have asked the waiter, but I wasn't really expecting to find the wind farm.

"I'm not sure. Something like seventy-five, maybe. You should step out here for a minute. It's pretty cool."

"Oh, sure. I probably won't have a chance like this again."

I open her door and carefully help her out. She uses my forearm for leverage.

"I bet Grandpa would have loved this. Being an engineer, he would like seeing these types of new developments."

"He would have loved it. There are so many things I wish he could have seen, Iain, things we could have talked about."

"Like a field of windmills."

"Exactly," she says.

I help Grandma around to the front of the car. She lets go of my arm and leans back on the hood, above the bumper. The few steps around the car have tired her. Her breaths are heavy and laboured.

"Before the war broke out, George had enrolled in university. But it was during the Great Depression, and after a couple of years he had to leave school because he couldn't afford tuition."

"What did he do then?"

"Well, he had to find work, but there wasn't much in those days. He decided to ride the freight cars. He'd jump on and jump off to try and work on farms. There were a lot of farms in those days, and he'd work as a helper, a farmhand. He used to say he was hungry during this time; work was sparse. That's really all he said about it. He said he didn't mind, but for some reason I hated thinking about him being hungry."

"But then war broke out overseas?"

"That's right. He enlisted in the navy. He was stationed on a minesweeper in the English Channel."

"Wasn't he some type of navigator?"

"Yup. It was a role he was good at; it suited him. And after the war, once we were married, we went out west."

"How come?"

"Originally we thought just for our honeymoon. We took the train from Winnipeg to Vancouver, then went on to Victoria. George wanted to stay at the fanciest hotel, the Empress. We couldn't afford it, though. And George was thinking maybe we should just stay out in Victoria and he would start a business."

"What kind of business?"

"I don't think he was sure. And I don't think that's what he really wanted to do, either. I remember sitting with him — this is so funny that I can remember this — and I knew he had to make up his own mind. No one could tell him what to do, but he always liked to talk about things. I just suggested that he go back and finish university. I told him I'd be happy to go back to work at the hospital. We could live off my salary."

"I didn't know you went back to work so soon after the war."

"Well, I'm getting to that. So anyway, he thought about it and, yes, he decided he'd like to go back to school. He went out and bought a huge book of mathematics to refresh his mind. He hadn't been studying in years. But I knew he could do it. I knew he was a smart guy. That summer, after he enrolled back in school for the fall, we stayed in Victoria. We obviously couldn't afford to stay in a hotel, so we found a cheap room to rent in a house. George took a job at the dockyards. The couple who owned the house also lived there. They gave us use of the kitchen and bathroom. It was all we needed and was very cheap. It was small but we loved it. It was only a short time, just one summer. I have such fond memories, Iain, even if I can't fully remember them. I'm not sure if that makes any sense, but it's true."

There's a natural break in our chat. It's the first true stop for a while and lasts full minutes, I would guess, not seconds.

"Well, it would have been an exciting time," I finally say. "The war was over, you'd just married. You could finally start your life."

"Everything changed on the train back to Winnipeg. I guess it really changed about six weeks before that. It was on the train that I told George I was pregnant. I'd been concerned about it, telling him, that is. You see, this was going to change our plans. I wouldn't be able to work because in those days if you were pregnant you had to stop working immediately. It was ridiculous, like so many things. But if I couldn't work, I wasn't sure George would be able to go back to school. I was worried he was going to be disappointed. And it wasn't like we were planning on it."

"Was he upset?"

Grandma has been playing with the bottom edge of her sweater. She stops now, looking up. "He was absolutely delighted. He really was thrilled. Back in Winnipeg my mom gave up her apartment and went to live with my sister Lottie. So we moved into her old place. George went to university and we lived off my small pension. And of course, his tuition was paid for by the government."

"How did it go?"

"We enjoyed those years. I remember lots of laughing. George was so absent-minded. Once, he was leaving the apartment very early because he had some work to do before class. In fact I was still in bed. About five minutes later I heard the door. And then George was back in the bedroom. I asked him what he'd forgotten this time. He just looked at me and then said, 'My shoes.' He'd left without his shoes." Grandma's laughing harder now. "Can you imagine that? It was typical George."

"So how did you get from that apartment in Winnipeg to Ottawa?"

"In his last year of school, George was always checking the job board to see if there were any postings for electrical engineers. He found one, a job with the government. It was in Ottawa. He applied for it and was offered the position. I didn't know this until later, but he wasn't sure if he wanted to take it. He didn't think I would want to leave Winnipeg, because my family was there. Even after he told me about it, he still wasn't sure. The first letter of response he wrote was to decline the job. He would find something else, something in Winnipeg. Then we talked some more and he wrote a second letter, an acceptance. He carried both letters with him to school every day, for weeks. Every night when he got home I'd ask which one he'd mailed. For a while he would always say neither. Until one day when he came home and put the rejection down on the table. We were going to be moving to Ottawa. I was thrilled. He knew that's what I wanted. It would be something new for both of us. A fresh start."

"Grandma, do you think it's strange that when my dad was my age, he was married, had children, his own home, several university degrees, a steady job, and also how his bed was a proper bed and not just a mattress on the floor?"

"Sorry, dear?"

That was a stupid question to put to her, out of the blue like that. I'd have to repeat it, and slow down for her to catch it.

"It's nothing important," I say. "I'm just thinking about how different things are now and how much different my life is at this stage than Dad's was or yours."

"It took me longer to do some of the things I wanted to do as well."

"Is time really best used as a contextual element for our lives?" I ask.

"Isn't it more something to appreciate and enjoy?" she responds.

"What?"

"Time," she says. "We shouldn't think of it as something we've already lost or are losing. Time helps us along. It actually makes things easier."

"You think?"

"Time can be made almost irrelevant in certain situations. Like when you're enjoying something. It seems to me," she says, "time is usually only a detrimental force when we're aware of it. It's like with breathing or your heart beating; better for those things to happen without us being aware. When you think about it too much, it will just throw you off."

I've been picking at the edge of a fingernail as Grandma speaks, listening. It finally breaks off.

"It is amazing how some people find them ugly," Grandma says.

"What?"

"The turbines," she explains, rising up off the hood gradually. She takes another look around her. "Maybe you have to get up close like this to appreciate them. Maybe they're just ugly to some people, you know, regardless of where they see them from."

WE PASS ONLY one car on our drive back to the ferry dock. We see more ducks than humans; three are swimming in an inlet, unconcerned as we slow to watch them. We have twenty minutes or so before our ride back, and when we see the general store we both agree that's where our loose change and those twenty minutes should be used up. We park and walk back along the road to the store.

Grandma's drawn in by the glistening sausages rotating on the stationary belt under bright warming lights. This is an unshakeable symptom of living through the Depression. Apart from the war, the Depression has had the largest impact on how Grandma experiences the world. Spinning preservative-filled meat in a store like this is attractive; there's just nothing she can do about it.

I'm less enchanted and begin my search for a suitable candy bar for the ride back. Something with peanuts and perhaps nougat, I think. Grandma eventually wanders off toward the back of the store.

"I just can't believe I found all these goodies here," she says, returning to the cash. "What a great store. It's so different."

I'm already half done my Snickers. Grandma holds up her booty: a pack of spearmint Life Savers, an individual pouch of microwave popcorn, and a dust-covered glass jar of ground paprika. "Are you sure you don't want to take a look back there? Lots of treats."

"I think I'm fine with this treat. We'd better get back to the car, anyway. Ferry will be loading now."

Thankfully, the rain has stayed away for our ride back. We take our place in the line of cars and snake our way on board. Again our view is of the walls of the ship and the other cars around us. I play the Guthrie tape. I yawn and close my eyes, and recline my seat an inch or two.

"You should take a nap," says Grandma. "Are you feeling okay?"

"Yeah, I'm fine. Just a little tired. I usually am at this time of day."

Grandma opens her window a crack and removes her seatbelt. "How are you sleeping these days?"

"Not bad, I guess. But I'm not a very good sleeper. I never have been. If I start thinking too much about anything, I can't sleep. I've just always been like that."

I tell Grandma about some of the things that have caused me restlessness over the years. Illness was one. Not as a threat to me necessarily, but to my family, friends, even pets. We lost a close family member to cancer when I was young. Another to complications after surgery. During those years I became fixated on death. I envisioned car accidents. Worrying became synonymous with going to bed.

"If Jimmy or Jean was out late, I'd just be lying on my side in bed, waiting to hear the engine and the gravel crunching under the tires. The dog would bark. The headlights would flash in through my blinds. Then maybe I could fall asleep.

"But it was during university when I started to worry about something less speculative."

"What was it?" asks Grandma.

"One night, I was standing at the toilet. Beside me, on the wall to my right, it looked like someone had scribbled some graffiti with a black Magic Marker. I couldn't decipher the lettering. Turns out it was an insect, one I'd never seen before.

"I was never into insects, but this one was particularly grotesque. Its torso was long and skinny, like a julienned vegetable, and it had very thin and long legs that looked like strands of human hair. It was the tentacles that really disgusted me," I say. Reliving this old story with Grandma has perked me up. I haven't thought of it in years. I'm no longer yawning.

"I've never seen a bug like that."

"Neither had I. I went down to the apartment below and asked the guys if I could borrow some type of aerosol spray — Raid, or whatever they had that would kill bugs. They just stayed on their sofa. The air smelled of recently used hot knives."

"Hot what?" asks Grandma.

"Hot knives."

"Oh, okay."

"They told me they had just the thing. They wondered half-heartedly what kind of bug. When I described in detail what I'd seen, they sat up. They recoiled. They told me it was a house centipede.

"It was the first time I'd ever heard that name, Grandma. I'd thought it was called a silverfish. They told me house centipedes actually *eat* silverfish. And other bugs, even spiders," I say. "For the next couple of years, every now and then it would come up: someone would mention a house centipede. More often not by name but by description.

"Then, one day, I was at a brunch party. My friend, an emergency physician, often entertained big groups at a time. As is often the case in a group of doctors, the line of discourse had taken a turn toward the medical. My friend was telling everyone about this very strange case she'd seen the night before, about this guy who came in complaining about some pain in his ear. Said it felt like a dull ache, thought he could feel something.

"My doctor friend continued, saying how she assumed he had some wax or an infection. She wasn't thinking it was going to be anything serious. But she decided to take a look. She was saying how everything was pretty much looking normal, but then she thought she saw something, an obstruction. She said it seemed like it was moving."

"Uh-oh," says Grandma.

"I remember setting my fork down. I started paying attention. She said it was pretty obvious there was something in there, something with legs, with lots of legs. She explained that he could feel something in there because there *was* something in there."

"I know what you're going to say," says Grandma, shaking her head, grimacing.

"Yup, she told us how it was 'one of those super-creepy bugs.' She said, 'One with all those legs.' I was thinking, *Dear God, of course I know.* And, *How dare you! Don't you dare say it.* But she did. She said, 'I think it's a type of centipede.' A few people nodded. Some chuckled. 'Yup, that's it,' she said. 'He had a centipede in his ear. It had crawled in during the night.'

"The story of that guy was the nail in my coffin. You see, I'd been reading in bed, a couple weeks earlier, when I felt something near my head, something very delicate. Probably nothing, I thought. I ignored it.

"When I felt a second, similar sensation, that of being caressed by a feather, across my eye — that would be EYE, part of my FACE — I shot straight up, reaching for my flashlight. Nothing. I pulled back the sheets, though, just to be sure . . . A house centipede the size of a small zucchini sprinted down toward my feet."

"Oh, no, in your bed?"

"I flung the covers to one side and barrel-rolled out of

the other side. It fled behind my bookcase," I say. "So when I left the brunch party, I headed home and called Jimmy. I was looking for some engineering tips, older-brother encouragement, anything to help secure my room. Or even just reassurance, that the story was a fluke, a one-off."

"A good idea," says Grandma. "I would have done the same."

"Jimmy told me that the story from brunch made sense because they love small, dark places, like pipes. Ears, noses, he said, there were lots of places they'd probably like to go. He did offer some practical advice, about moving my bed away from the wall and putting each of its legs in a container filled with water, which would likely be a strong enough deterrent.

"The problem was there were no legs to put in water. My bed was just a worn mattress on a box spring. On the floor. So I pulled the bed out from the wall. Then I moved onto the next phase — scent dissuasion."

"What's that?"

"It was just an idea I came up with to try and keep them away. I figured that most insects were sensitive to strong scents. I gathered anything I thought might apply — old soap cartons and dryer sheets were ideal. I put them all around my bed."

"I thought I saw some soap boxes around your bed the other day," says Grandma. "I wondered why but didn't say anything."

"When Mom called to see how things were going one night, I told her about what was happening. How I was going crazy. She offered her own suggestion of salt. She said

I should sprinkle it around my bed. She didn't think they'd like getting the sharp salt pieces in their legs. And then she started getting really excited. She suggested some herbs: dried, not fresh; maybe some basil, oregano, or, better yet, cayenne or smoked paprika. I wasn't sold, but I had some herbes de Provence, so I sprinkled it liberally."

"Oh, Iain."

"Funnily enough, it was a light that finally let me doze. It was the one I'd had with me since I was a kid. It's a chicken-shaped night light that plugs directly into a wall socket."

"I saw that, too," says Grandma, smiling.

"Yeah, I found it in one of my desk drawers," I say. "So this is basically how I sleep every night now, pushed away from the wall, ear-plugged, surrounded by strong synthetic scents, dried herbs, and a small chicken torch spraying its light across half the room. And if it's not centipedes, I'm often thinking of something. I might start thinking of all the moments in a day when it's possible to choke on food or catch a foot and fall down some stairs. Other nights I think about something completely arbitrary, like a bag of brown sugar with an image on the front of a steaming cup of coffee. I'll think about how that was someone's job, to design the brown sugar bag. Why did they decide to put the steaming mug of coffee on it? None of this makes sense or is even reasonable, I know."

"It's just the way your mind works. I wish I could be more of a help," adds Grandma, patting me on the arm. "But you know me, I never have any problem with sleep."

"That's amazing. It doesn't even rattle you when you're away from home or in another bed?"

"It doesn't even need to be a bed," she says. "I can always sleep."

The lack of rain, and maybe all the chatting, has made for a more pleasant trip back to the mainland. My mouth is dry from talking so much.

"That really is amazing," I say. "Sometimes when I can't sleep, I'm not sure if it's because of something I was already thinking about too much or because I start worrying about not sleeping.

"I have a self-imposed rule," I say. "If I've been lying there for more than an hour, I have to stop checking the clock. It only makes it worse if I keep looking and confirming how late it's getting. So I just try and ignore it. Sometimes I end up reading until it starts to get light out."

"I haven't been awake at that time of night for ages."

I turn down the Guthrie tape. "When you go to bed, how do you just turn your mind off?"

"Well," she says, "I guess I don't have to."

I look out my window for a bit and then ask Grandma if she wants to go up to the observation deck. But she says she's happy to stay in the car; she might even take a little snooze.

8:14 p.m.

I TOLD GRANDMA I would make dinner.

"Oh, are we staying in to eat tonight?" she asked.

"Yeah. It's our last night. I thought that would be nice."

"It'll be great."

I poured her a glass of sherry and marshalled her to her pink chair, where she could read until dinner.

I returned to the kitchen and exhaled audibly. I put on my apron and made a scratch meatloaf with the lamb from the farm. I mixed the lamb with breadcrumbs, garlic, onion, an egg, and some spices, including cumin and cinnamon, and topped it with a sweet-and-sour sauce I made by reducing ketchup, vinegar, mustard, and brown sugar. I boiled some frozen peas and made a quick salad with iceberg lettuce, with mashed potatoes to go along. I understand it may not sound appealing to most, but this type of meat-and-potatoes dinner is right up Grandma's alley. It's the type of dinner she would have made for her family. She's always saying how she doesn't need anything fancy.

The loaf took some time to cook. It was after 7:30 p.m. by the time we sat. Now it's after 8 p.m., and we're just finishing. Grandma claimed to enjoy it. I think I was a bit heavy-handed with the cumin. She says she wants the recipe.

"And tell me again what you did with the salad. What was the dressing?" She takes a scrap piece of paper and a small blue pencil from her purse. "I want to write this down."

"It's very easy. Just some balsamic, oil, and mustard. And just mix it all together. It's called Iain's Special Dressing."

"It was lovely."

Grandma's been doing this with most things I've made. She's asked for the recipe and then written it down. I don't imagine she'll ever get around to making any of these dishes. She thinks she will. I'm not sure she'll remember she's written them down or even be able to find them, since some are just on scraps of paper. But it shows how much she still enjoys food and the idea of cooking. It's knee-bucklingly charming.

"I've always liked food," she says.

"Yeah, I've noticed that. It's great you still enjoy eating."

"I've had some wonderful meals in my life. I've forgotten most of them by now."

"But there are obviously some you remember."

It takes her a moment to calibrate her thoughts. She places her notepaper on the table. "There was something I ate in Rome," she says.

She tells me that in Rome, as in London, she seldom went anywhere or did anything alone. "Not by choice," she says. "There was always a soldier, another nurse, a group around to join whatever was happening. One day I'd decided to go for a walk down into the city. I'm not sure how or why, but I was alone. It was a rare stroll, to have some privacy.

"We never really had much meat, and our rations were rarely satisfying. I'd been eating a lot of dry biscuits. The Americans had better rations. The Canadian nurses were given British supplies. When lucky, I would sometimes share a luxury only the Americans were given."

"What was that?" I ask.

"Spam. The canned Spam was ambrosial. And at this point I hadn't had any Spam in months. I remember I was very hungry," she says.

I stand and clear our plates. I leave the wineglasses. There's still about a third of the bottle left.

"I'm still listening," I confirm, carrying the plates to the sink.

"Even for us nurses, clean water was very limited. The strict rationing included assigned canteens. We had to find the water truck in the morning to fill up. We had to use it for drinking, but also cleaning our teeth, washing, everything."

Grandma tells me she had a German water bottle and had started using it. She doesn't reveal how she got it. "But the German design was superior. It had a larger volume and a cup attached to the top."

She tells me again how she'd always loved food and eating. She'd grown up in a family who all appreciated and delighted in their nightly meal. She reminds me of this, but having seen her clean her plate entirely, even at ninety-two, at every meal this week, I'm keenly aware of her love of food and eating. She is wonderfully unfinicky.

"Back before the war, it was common while I was still studying in Winnipeg to stop on my way home to pick up some supplies for supper. I knew where to go: the basement of the Hudson's Bay store. They had a deli and fish counter down there. It was one of my favourite places in the city.

"I knew the men who worked there. I recognized the smells. Occasionally, as a treat, my mother would request a piece of cheese. My father's preference was always Gorgonzola.

"When I was younger still, my standard school lunch consisted of bread, butter, and a can of sardines. My classmates were always grossed out. I loved those lunches. And every so often, my mom would pack a piece of cheese."

Grandma explains how it was cheese of all sorts that was the creamy, savoury foundation, the family's comfort food, at any meal. "We all just absolutely craved cheese," she says before pausing. Her expression changes. "What was I telling you about?"

"You were talking about going for a walk one day, in Rome. And you were alone."

"Yes, yes, I'm sorry, that's right," she says. "When I was away from my duties, away from the routine, that's when I was hungriest."

Grandma had gone for a solo swim in the sea. Then, she says, she went for a stroll. She found a signless café and entered.

"From the size and layout I assumed it served coffee, tea, maybe some sweets. But once I got inside, where I could smell all the smells, I realized it was a real restaurant. The waiter was a middle-aged man. He was tall and thin, like a fencepost.

"He moved around casually, gently, on the balls of his feet. I guessed he was in his late forties, but he looked older. I think he nodded at me when I first came in, smiled maybe, and left me some more time to settle in. He'd recognized my nursing uniform so was happy to serve me."

"Even though he was Italian?" I ask.

"Yes, definitely. It seemed like everyone I met in Rome was happy to see me. It was amazing. I was welcomed everywhere in the city. Since being in Sicily and Italy, I'd sort of generalized everyone as lovers, not fighters. I know it sounds silly, but that's just how I felt. Like us, they wanted the war to end.

"Before I got to the café, I passed a young teenager on the street who was humming. So I kind of lingered within earshot. And I recognized the tune. Unlike the boys of that age in Canada, he was humming an operatic song. You see, it was just different there."

"I'm sure."

"I actually thought the waiter looked like an older version of the humming boy. Maybe it was his father. Probably not. But maybe. The waiter had been humming, too. Maybe that's why I thought they looked alike."

Grandma laughs, I think at the implausibility of the two being related. It takes a moment for her to regain her place in the story.

"The place was empty. The street had been busy, and I could see people walking by the window. I suppose the majority of locals probably wouldn't have had any money to spend in a restaurant.

"It was cool inside; I think the window had been opened slightly. I could feel very little breeze, if any. I felt so comfortable. And as soon as I sat down I knew what I wanted. I'd been craving it for weeks, Iain, months. Well, for years."

"What?"

"If the waiter had told me they served the freshest, best-tasting pasta on earth, smothered in the most exquisite sauce, I would have believed him. It just felt like the kind of place where a claim like that could be true. I could smell coffee and imagined it was likely better than any coffee I'd ever had. But I didn't want pasta or coffee.

"You see," she continues, "being treated wasn't uncommon in those days. It just rarely involved food. It was often drink. One time — you can stop me if I've told you this already — I was taken to a pub — have I told you this?"

"No, I don't think so."

"I was with a pilot. He was tall, a basketball player. I used to tell him that after the war I was going to have five children and all five would be boys. I wanted a family. He didn't know why I wanted five boys. I just thought five boys would be fun.

"But at the pub we met up with a large group. He left me at the table and returned with two glasses. Each one had a couple of inches of dark amber liquid. He put one down in front of me." Grandma mimics the action of putting a glass down in front of her, her empty hand landing with a thud on the table. "And he kept one for himself. Just as he sat down, I picked up the glass, brought it up to my mouth, and tipped it down in one go. *Whoosh*, just like that." She brings her hand up to her mouth, throws her head back, and then lets her hand fall back down to the table.

"It burned all the way down. He was shocked. You should have seen his face. He wasn't expecting me to drain it in one go. He asked me if I knew how much it had cost. He went on to tell me it was fine cognac. He said I was meant to swirl it, to sniff it, to sip it. I just shrugged and told him I was sorry. But it was pretty funny. He went back and got me another. But why was I telling you this?"

"You were telling me about the restaurant where you went alone."

"Yes, that's right. In the restaurant that day I didn't want wine or cognac. And I was going to treat myself. I was alone, it was up to me. This will probably sound ridiculous to you, Iain, but you know what I wanted? Just cheese. And I wanted it plain, with a piece of fresh white bread."

I'm watching Grandma as she speaks. Her cheeks have reddened again as the evening has advanced. Likely from the wine, though perhaps she's tired from the day, and the talking, maybe her cold. She looks happy, though. She looks lively, awake.

"It doesn't sound ridiculous at all, Grandma," I answer. "I can't relate, obviously, but I can imagine."

"But it was trying to order that became a game of mis-understanding. The waiter's English was poor. And as you know, language has never been my strength. Eventually, in my fuzzy, broken Italian, I conveyed my simple request. I just wanted some cheese, any cheese. He was genuinely pleased when he finally understood. Five minutes later he was back carrying two plates."

"And you were still alone in the place?"

"Yup, just the waiter and me. One plate had crusty bread, the other had the cheese. He didn't tell me what kind. He just smiled and left it on the table.

"I knew I'd come to the right place, because the bread was warm. The piece was thick and crusty; I ripped it in two with my hands. The cheese was light in colour, a cloudy beige that grew lighter around the edges. I smelled it. It had an earthy, salty scent. It was firm. I wasn't really concerned about this, though. I wanted to taste it. I broke off a hunk and put it on top of the bread and took a bite. I've never had another bite of food like it. Never.

"After the war, thousands of miles from the restau-rant in Rome, that meal came up for the first time. I told my Italian neighbour about the only piece of cheese I ate throughout the war. It had stayed in my mind. It came up the way these things do, spontaneously. It was summer. We were both outside working in our gardens, talking over the fence. My hands and knees were covered in dirt. I had mud under my fingernails, my cheeks must have been beet red, I was hot and sweaty. And I described the cheese in detail to him. I'm still not sure how it came up.

"He figured it was probably Romano. But not like the Romano you get in Canada. And I think he was probably right, but I'll never know for sure. It's funny, I still buy Romano every now and then, when I see it, just to see what it tastes like. I can't help myself."

Grandma pauses and looks up at me. "And look, I'm telling you about a piece of cheese from all those years ago. I didn't need to tell you all that, did I? It was just a piece of cheese." She shakes her head, takes a sip of wine, and looks away. "You probably think I'm crazy."

I'VE FILLED UP our glasses for the last time. We've drained the bottle. Tonight, 750 millilitres aren't enough. One of the tea lights on the table has burned out. I have some replacements in a drawer and am up to get one. "It's a nice wine, isn't it?" she adds. "Not that I know much about wine."

"Yeah, I like Beaujolais. Except for the fact that my lips get all stained."

"Are they stained? I hadn't noticed."

I noticed my tarnished lips in the window by the sink when I got up to retrieve the candle. Even in this faint light, it's hard to miss. "My lips tend to stain easily," I say. "Yours are fine. Maybe you have stain-resistant lips."

"Oh, really?" She looks at me quizzically and grins. "You know, I've never really thought about that."

We laugh, we sip. Of course she hasn't.

Along with her reflections, we've covered a wide range of topics, including politics and sports. But as I've been noticing the past couple of days, regardless of where we start or where we emerge, Grandma has been returning to her family.

Her brother Donald has come up a few times this week. But she's never stayed on the topic long enough to give many details about his own wartime experience. I leave the remains of supper on the plate for now and ask about Donald.

"Well, you know he was a pilot?"

"Yeah, I knew that. Didn't he get shot down?" I catch a whiff of the remaining meatloaf left in the pan. I'm almost feeling hungry again. If I'd made a dessert, now would be the perfect time for it.

"He did, yes, several times. Five in total."

"Really?"

"Yes, and the fourth time, his plane crashed behind German lines. He was found shortly after the crash and was picked up by a Bedouin tribe. They spoke no English but were able to communicate with him just enough for each to understand the other. They were sympathetic and wanted to help. He definitely wouldn't have survived without them," she says. "They cared for him. They removed his torn uniform. They had to dress him like one of their own so he wouldn't stand out. They darkened his face with ash from the fire. Their only concern was his eyes. Donald had very deep blue eyes."

"How long did he stay with them?"

"Long enough to heal. He was grateful, but once he regained some strength he wanted to get back to the Allied lines. His plane was beyond repair. They agreed to shepherd him for the entire route. It took five days and five nights to get back."

We're both quiet, withdrawing into our own thoughts.

Grandma breaks the silence. "There were lots of reasons why Donald and I were so close, I think. I knew him as well as any sister could know a brother," she says. "He wasn't a fighter, not like me. One day at school, this was when I was a teenager, I was looking out the window. I saw Donald; he was being chased by two bullies. They were older and bigger. I didn't know why they were after him. But he never fought. I watched him run to a tree and climb up. And they were still there, waiting for him to come down. I wasn't listening to the lesson anymore. I was glaring out toward the field, the tree. I wished he would climb down and fight. I really wanted to get up, leave the classroom, walk outside, and fight them myself. I just wanted to get at them."

I can't help but laugh at this. I believe her, though.

"I don't think I've ever told you about this one day overseas," she says. "It had been a pretty quiet day at the hospital. It had been hot for weeks. This was the hottest day yet."

Grandma tells me that even on days off, it was rare not to be occupied with something of tangible or emotional significance. But the wind was dead, the air was muted, plants looked plastic, and dirt seemed fake. On those days of heat and inactivity, Grandma became unglued from routine. Those were days without goals or tasks. Verve and ambition, like the breeze, were dormant.

"So I'd left my room without aim. I just felt like being outside. I was restless and wanted to feel the sun and heat, I guess. I didn't immediately recognize him. It was easy to approach strangers at the hospital; they were typically happy to chat. This airman was no different. I generally liked pilots because of the connection to Donald. So I just went up to this pilot and we talked, just chit-chat. But for some reason I couldn't resist mentioning how I had a younger brother who was a pilot.

"The man wondered where Donald was stationed. I told him with 450 Squadron. They were in the desert. It was almost like the man recoiled slightly; his expression changed. He told me that wasn't true. I told him I didn't understand. Right away he started laughing and apologized. He didn't mean I was wrong, just that I wasn't properly up to date. He explained how 450 Squadron wasn't in the desert.

"'They aren't?' I say. 'How do you know?' According to him they were now in Sicily. I can still picture his face when he told me that," she says. "I really couldn't believe it. I knew it would be unlikely, but it meant there was a chance I might be able to get in touch with someone who would know something of Donald's whereabouts. Even if it was just to hear he was well from someone who knew. That would have meant everything to me.

"I thanked the pilot for the chat and his news. I continued my walk with a purpose now. I was excited, so I took a little detour just to clear my head. I found the matron of my hospital outside her office, in the hallway. She was already talking with someone, a soldier. When I got close enough, I saw he was a high-ranking British officer. Regardless of the topic or how casual they seemed or how important my question was, this wasn't a conversation I should barge in on. I had to wait.

"I stopped a few feet away. I was probably bouncing on the balls of my feet or fidgeting my hands. I'm not sure; I was trying to keep it together."

Grandma, the keeper of serenity, undeniably unruffle-able, says she was aware of the beating heart in her chest.

"As the matron carried on, I would have done anything to grab her attention. But I kept waiting. It must have been two or three minutes before she noticed me. She looked surprised to see one of her nurses standing there. She wondered what I wanted."

Being enormously excited makes the most mundane and manageable actions formidable. Grandma must have had to think carefully about what she was saying, to keep her enthusiasm in check. She must have had electric bones.

"I told them what I'd just heard, that it was a long shot, but that my younger brother, or someone connected to him, might be in Sicily. I was trying to sound calm. It was the officer, not the matron, who answered. He wondered which squadron. I told him. I think he looked back toward the matron for a flash. Then he told me it was true, that squadron was in Sicily. He knew it because they had just arrived with an Australian squadron. He pointed off to his right. He said they were just down the road."

In a war like that, minute increments of time could often carry immense potency. The fundamentals of a life, or lives, regularly veer in a second. Emotion doesn't have a chance to yield to retrospection. Grandma tells me that what she was experiencing was a blend of extreme surprise, aggressive elation, and total warmth. What were the odds he was still with them? That he wasn't hurt, or worse? But at least she might be able to get some information, an update.

"Remember, I hadn't seen or talked to Donald in years. Before the officer left, he said he wasn't sure how likely it was, but if Donald was still with them, maybe I could try to track him down. He told me it would have to wait until the next day."

Grandma takes a break for a sip of wine. I'm sure the concept of tomorrow was as close to indecipherable as such a normal word could be. It must have lost its meaning. It must have been strangely difficult to interpret when tomorrow would become today.

"I returned to my room. I sat down on my cot. I'd been sewing. It's funny, because I'd never been much of a sewer. But I kept on sewing. I had to do something. I had to be busy. I couldn't tell you how long I'd been at it when another nurse appeared at my door. She was beaming. 'Nick!' she called to me. 'It's your brother! He's downstairs!'"

Grandma's voice has been steady and consistent throughout the entire story. She hasn't been muddled or stumbled at all. She's been clear and solid. And not just for someone who is ninety-two. She's been objectively steady, clear. But it's here, when she says, "He's downstairs," that there's a noticeable change, a variation in pitch. She has to pause and clear her throat before she can continue.

"Even though the nurse was excited and had yelled the news, I heard it perfectly. I absorbed it. But I didn't freeze. Instead I leaped up. I threw the sewing to my left onto the floor, or somewhere, I didn't see where it landed. I rushed past her and ran out of the room. I ran down the long corridor.

"I was told the full story later. The British officer who'd been talking with the matron had gone down the road, looking for Donald. And somehow he'd found him. He told Donald what had happened, who he'd talked with, that he'd just met this nurse. He offered Donald his own motorcycle. He told him to be quick, but he'd better go up and say hi to his big sister. Imagine, lending out his own motorcycle.

"I ran the entire way, all the way to the stairwell, and just continued running down the stairs. I had three flights to get down. When I got to the last flight of steps, I could see outside. There at the bottom of the stairs was this lanky figure, a few feet away, a boy. I never would have known that I could recognize his posture, but I could. Just the way he was standing, I knew it was him. And just for a moment, maybe a few seconds, I looked at him."

For the first time on our trip, Grandma's voice breaks. It's the first time in all her stories, all her reflections, that she's forced to stop because of emotion. She shakes her head and smiles. She looks down, then up. Her eyes have filled up and she wipes at them gently with the back of her index finger. She takes a few moments to compose herself.

"He was dressed in khaki shorts and worn boots. He was wearing an Australian airman's hat. I can still see him standing there. I'd never seen him so tanned. He looked older, but still so young. He was so thin, and all covered in dust.

"I started to run again, down the last flight. I took the first step, but then I just jumped. I had to. I went right over the last five and landed at the bottom. I grabbed him and hugged him. I thought I could detect some commotion. We'd caused a scene. I didn't care. Somewhere behind me, I heard someone scream when I jumped. It wasn't proper conduct for a nurse. Then I definitely heard a second voice telling the screamer it was okay, it was fine. That that boy was my little brother."

9:55 p.m.

INSTEAD OF HER lips, the wine has made her face redder still, a shade that, I think, is even brighter in contrast to her white hair. Grandma's up out of her chair. She's shuffling to the right and then the left. Her hands are down almost as low as her knees.

After the dishes — me washing, her drying — we opted to move to the (relatively) comfortable chairs. That's when I remembered my liquor store purchase, the one I'd run back in to get: that bottle of Southern Comfort Grandma had commented on. She seemed thrilled to see it. It was the least I could do.

Her enthusiasm was preceded by a moment of communal confusion. Neither of us knew the best way to consume this amber liquid. Grandma couldn't remember. She did recount her story again, about her and Grandpa taking a trip together — she'd forgotten she'd already told me. I'm not sure if she realized that was why I bought it.

I used my computer to find the most common drinks made with Southern Comfort. I was instructed to mix it with some fresh lime juice and serve over ice.

Once I was on the couch and Grandma was in her pink chair, we held up our cups for a moment until she suggested we toast the trip. It was a pleasingly sour drink. But sweet, too. In itself, an appropriate metaphor for what we were toasting.

My line of questioning turned to her life in the early twenties. It's an era I'm interested in and have read extensively about. Some of my favourite books are set in and around the twenties. But up until this week, I've never spent much time talking to her about it. This is what led to her getting up out of her chair.

To do her dance performance.

It's her rendition of the Charleston, the defining dance of the time. It was the early years of jazz, when ragtime was still prevalent. We've been listening to jazz all night. Count Basie, Bessie Smith, and Benny Goodman.

She can't continue her performance for long. After thirty seconds or so she's out of breath, like she was on Wolfe Island. She dances for another ten seconds, and when she falls back into the chair her pant leg comes up. I notice something black around her upper shin. She notices me looking.

"Oh, it's nothing. Just one of those braces."

"You're wearing a brace? For your knee?"

"Yeah, I'm supposed to be wearing it whenever I walk around. So I thought I should throw it into my bag for the trip. I'm not sure it does a whole lot."

"Have you been wearing it much?"

"Some of the time." This probably means most of the time; she would never say.

"I didn't know your leg was still bugging you." It's the injury from the fall she had outside her hair salon. "You haven't said anything."

"Oh, no, it's not, really. It's silly, really. I'm lucky it hasn't gotten any worse."

She extends her leg and rolls up her pants. It's a firm nylon brace. It's hard to believe I haven't noticed it until now, the last night of our vacation. She's holding her leg straight out and up off the floor. I grab the stool from under my own heavy leg.

"Here, you should have had this all along. How's it feeling?"

"Fine. Much better today. There's definitely an improvement. I'll need all my parts working for next week."

"How come?"

"I've agreed to be part of an art installation. It sounds quite interesting."

"What is it?"

"A French artist is putting together an exhibit called *Resistance*. He's going to take photos of body parts of several veterans from the war. He's going to blow each picture up very big and display it alongside a very small picture of the face of the same vet taken around the time of the war."

"That does sound cool. Do you know what body part he'll take?"

"No, but I don't really care. Whatever he suggests. I imagine some will have an idea of what they want. I bet some won't want to show certain parts. Maybe I'll suggest my legs or feet; he probably won't have many of those. Old feet aren't pretty."

We talk some more about the installation and other commitments Grandma has for the coming weeks. There are many. She has invitations to dinners and parties; her weekly golf games are starting up soon. There's so much she's still engaged in, so much she still thinks about.

As our glasses empty, we start to yawn. Grandma first and then me. We ignore the yawns initially, hiding them with our hands.

"I guess it's that time again," says Grandma over the music. "But what a wonderful dinner. And a wonderful day. Thank you."

"No, thank you, Grandma. You treated. Again."

"I seem to talk more with you than with anyone. I'm sorry for going on and on. But it's been so nice to just reminisce this week. To think about old times. It's amazing what we can remember from so long ago."

"I like our chats," I say. "It's good to talk about these things. It's good for me."

"Well, I'm going to take my reading up to bed."

She smiles again and rocks herself in her seat three or four times. She needs to build this momentum to stand. I rise to help but she's up before I can give her my hand. She takes it anyway and pulls me in for a hug. I have to bend down low to accept it. I can feel her hand lightly tapping my shoulder blade, over and over.

"Thanks," she says again. At the door, she turns back. "What was the wine we had tonight?"

"Beaujolais."

"Oh, right. And what was that drink called again?"

"Southern Comfort," I say, "with lime juice."

"Right, Southern Comfort," she says. "If you're going to bed, too, then I'll get the lights out here."

"Yup, I'll be headed off soon."

"Goodnight."

"Nighty-night."

I watch her move gingerly over to the lamp. She twists the switch three times in the wrong direction, *click-click-click*, before reversing it, *click*. The room is dark.

"I've had such a wonderful week. I really have," I hear from the hall. "I've been thinking about so many things."

"Me, too. Have a good sleep, Grandma."

"You know you don't have to say that," she says. "I always do."

FRIDAY

7:55 a.m.

I WAKE EFFORTLESSLY, minutes before my alarm. I have a stretch, pointing my toes and hands in opposite directions. Despite a dry mouth that gives the impression I nibbled on a late-night bowl of hamster food, I feel well rested and alert. I don't linger in the sheets, delaying the compulsory, as I do most mornings. I'm up. I'm dressed.

I slept heavily. It was one of those nights that seemed to last for only a minute or two. Sometimes it's possible to be aware of time even while asleep. Not last night. I have only an obscure recollection of getting up off the couch and finding my way to bed in the dark. Unusually for me, I went straight to sleep. The longer the night feels, the worse the sleep. This was a good sleep, a great one. The night flew by.

It's in this state, feeling fresh, still basking in post-sleep gusto, that I find Grandma already in the kitchen. I can only see half of her, behind the table. It's her feet, toes pointing upward, that I see first. Her inert legs are next.

Grandma's on the floor. She's flat on her back.

I freeze a few feet from the threshold. My pulse quickens to a higher gear. Most people would rush in right at this moment. I'm still. What I am going to find? I have to go in.

She might need help. She might be hurt. I walk skittishly into the kitchen and around the table, which is distorting my view.

"Good morning," she says, with a beaming grin. Her face appears restored and comfortable; gone is the redness from last night. "How did you sleep?"

I exhale in relief, choking on the breath. "I actually slept really great."

"Oh, good. Happy to hear it. I thought you might."

"Grandma, what are you doing on the floor?" I ask.

"I was feeling better this morning. I think the worst of my cold is done. So I just thought I'd do some exercises and stretching. I guess it probably looks silly. I often do this at home. I've been feeling lazy since I've been here."

She pulls one leg into her chest as far as she can. She holds it there. Then brings the other leg, the one with the bad knee, up beside it. She can't get it quite as far. Beside her on the floor I notice a ball of bedsheets.

"But isn't the floor hard? Doesn't it hurt your back?"

"No, I like the wood floor. It's good for my back."

The spare bed has probably been murderous on her back. It is on mine. I should have switched beds. I should have taken the spare bed myself. But she would have insisted I stay in my own room. It's delusional to think otherwise. Still, I could have at least suggested it.

"I hope it's not the damn bed that's hurt your back."

"No, of course not, my back is fine. I enjoy doing these exercises. It's good for me."

I watch her release one leg, then the other. She just lies there on the floor. She puts her arms back behind her head and closes her eyes.

"How about a little breakfast, then, when you're done."

"Thanks, but I already had some, dear. I was up early. And I stripped the bed." She motions toward the ball of sheets beside her.

I thought I was up early?

I pull out one of the chairs from the table and flop down. Grandma continues her stretching. In the reflection in the window I can see my own distended tummy. I slap my belly twice and roll my neck on my shoulders, joining in on the morning calisthenics. The rain was supposed to have stopped. It hasn't. Not even for our last day. It's grey and raining and windy and generally shitty, like it's been for most of the past four days.

"Could you have some coffee, then? I'm going to make some."

"Coffee would be great."

As I prepare our brew, Grandma slowly rises up off the floor. It's a struggle. I want to ask if she needs any help, but I know by now she'd rather do it on her own, even if it takes longer.

"I was thinking about our dinner last night before I fell asleep," she says when she's up and seated at the table. "It was delicious, Iain. I can't believe how well we've eaten. I'm going to try and make that salad when I get home. I wrote down the recipe, right?"

"Yeah, you did. You had a little piece of paper with you. I think it's here somewhere."

I start shuffling through the newspapers, magazines, and notepaper scattered on the table beside the phone. I'm not convinced I'm going to find anything. "Here, I think this is it." I try not to sound too surprised. I hold up a white sticky note with what appears to be her handwriting. It's tricky to decipher. The writing, although neat and orderly, is small and unsteady. It doesn't look like a recipe. It's definitely her writing, though. "Maybe this isn't it."

"May I see?"

I pass the paper to Grandma. She accepts it and holds it up close to her face, squinting at her own writing. "No, this isn't the recipe. I'm not sure what ... Oh, I know what this is." She looks up, giggles, then turns back to the note. "It's mine, all right."

"What is it?"

"It's just a little diary, I guess. I decided on Tuesday I should start writing down what we've been doing. I knew if I didn't, I'd forget it. And some of it I want to remember."

I'm unexpectedly touched by this development. She's been keeping her own travelogue of our road trip — our road trip without a road, or a trip. On scrap paper. In faint pencil. I tell her I've had the same idea, that I've been doing the same thing. "I've been keeping some notes, too."

"I'll be able to read it over every now and then. It'll be nice to have."

I stand up and walk toward the sink. I've had the ingredients for peanut butter cookies sitting on the counter for more than a week. I was going to have the cookies ready for when Grandma arrived. That way my place would smell like fresh baking when we stepped inside. It never happened. I've been estranged from any desire to bake since the last time I baked a pie. It was also my first time, and the insides of the pecan filling came out like soup. I ate it (with a spoon) but wouldn't have wanted to serve it to anyone else. I know cookies are easier but I just couldn't do it. Now would have been a good time to offer Grandma a homemade cookie.

"Would you like to nibble on something with your coffee, Grandma?"

"No, dear. I think I'll wait until lunch."

WHEN IT COMES to weekday lunch in downtown Kingston, there are several choices. There are delis, lots of sushi, pizza. There are homemade takeout meals at a small grocery on Barrie Street. But when I feel like spending more money than I should, the bakery on Princess Street is nonpareil. The combination of fresh ingredients, extensive choice, and friendly service equates to an eternally packed interior and the diametric opposite of my kitchen.

The clientele are a blend of businesspeople, post-boomer artisans, grad students, and elderly retirees. The sum is an undissolved potion of affluent bread-and-soup-lovers. Grandma asked about the bakery when she saw it from the café, so I felt like I should take her to see it.

Walking along Princess Street today, what's noticeable is some of the empty buildings where there used to be stores. Along with the Starbucks, two burger joints, a shoe store, a dollar store, a chain drug store, a natural foods store, a cellphone retailer, and a couple of clothing stores, I count three empty buildings with paper half-covering their windows.

We pass a place where I used to buy books. It was called the Book Market. Someone has literally X-ed out the word

Book and scrawled *Art* above it. I guess it's now the Art Market. A number of the storefronts are festooned with flashy reminders of low prices and great deals. Grandma comments on the shoe store and wonders if it's new. It's not. I tell her new stores downtown have had a rough go lately and there are fewer and fewer new anythings.

We walk through the bakery's door to the unmistakable scent of fresh sourdough. I like it here but am already ruing the decision. I know she loves a satisfying soup-and-sammy lunch, but the bakery is more hectic than I thought it would be. Maybe I should have picked another place. We could have just grabbed takeout somewhere and eaten in my car. There's an urgency built into the glass display here. Everyone but us has things to do and places to go. All are in a hurry. Even the old people and lackadaisical students are in a hurry to get their lunches and go. The staff are extremely friendly and helpful but are taught to trump congeniality with efficiency. Most days I'm fine with this, but today it adds another layer of unwanted intensity.

The guy beside me is probably a student, or he could be about to depart on a month-long trek through the Andes. His backpack is holding more belongings than I own. There are water bottles and keys and frying pans dangling off many large buckles. I've just caught a glimpse of his face. He looks like he hasn't just smoked *from* a bong but has smoked the whole thing, drunk the water, and eaten the bong, too. The whites of his eyes are the colour of canned salmon.

Grandma's waiting unassumingly, holding her purse over her left shoulder. To her right is an elderly woman in a rain hat. She has a piece of notepaper with her. She's reading a list of orders from her paper to one of the women behind the counter. Beside her is a standard-issue insurance salesman, or banker, or real estate agent — clean-shaven; dark suit; short, neatly combed and gelled salt-and-pepper hair. Apart from large-scale coastal oil spills, is there anything worse and more unsettling in our world than the use of cologne? Not the overuse, just the use. Doesn't it seem like an antiquated measure, useful perhaps if we didn't have access to three-dollar sticks of deodorant and warm running water? And soap. We don't smell that terrible, do we, that we need to spray these repulsive chemicals onto our necks and then stand in line at a deli counter trying to decide between roast beef and pastrami while discharging the powerfully synthetic pheromone of a Glade Plug-In?

"Do you know what you're going to get?" asks Grandma.

I'm flustered. I turn and look at her. I have to stop myself from asking if she wants to go somewhere else, away from other humans. There has to be a restaurant around here with good food. And no other customers. "No, not for sure, what about you?"

"I'm thinking of just getting some cheese. And maybe one of those fresh croissants."

We've come at feeding time, but our goal should be to graze. There's a café in the back, and I suggest to Grandma we go back there and sit where we can eat slowly, without feeling rushed. It feels like the right place to go. We can eat our lunch at our own pace.

We find a square table for two beside a table for four. Most customers take their food out, so the café section is only a quarter full, at most.

I always try and decide what I want before I arrive. It's seemingly inevitable that I change my mind six or seven times before I place my order. And the split-second post-order is when I start to feel guilty for buying lunch at all. I should have just had peanut butter on toast at home.

Today I'm feeling rested and adventurous. I'm determined to make it a guilt-free lunch, for Grandma's sake. I want something I've never had. Maybe something open-faced or something with chorizo. The waiter drops off two coffees, water, and some fresh butter and bread and says he'll be back to take our orders.

"Looks pretty good, doesn't it?" I say.

"It does."

For a while we snack on the bread and butter, not talking much. The waiter returns and takes our order. We're going to share a grilled cheese and a café salad with roasted pumpkin seeds. The food arrives promptly and has already been split in two. We stop to rest after I'm done almost half my plate; Grandma is only three bites into hers. She unwinds the scarf from her neck and sets it down on the empty seat beside her.

"This is what's nice about getting old, being somewhere like this."

"Really?" I look around the café and back toward the busy bakery section.

"Everyone knows the bad parts about aging. We hear about them all the time. But I never could have guessed at any point in my life that I'd still be here, at this age, eating a green salad with pumpkin seeds with my grandson," she says. "I've been thinking about this, how the more you age, the older you get, the more of the future you get to see."

"I guess you're right," I say.

Patrons from two other tables have finished and left. Besides us, there's only one other occupied table now, under the "Specials" chalkboard across the room. It's an elderly lady, sitting alone. She's eating a bowl of soup and reading the paper.

I've often heard the cliché about how childhood comes full circle. We're born helpless and dependent; we grow, we age, and we die helpless. There are strands connecting the two. A child needs my help carrying heavy things like bags; so does Grandma. But really, childhood and old age are distinct stages. Grandma is right.

No age is a destination, just a place we are actively travelling through. Childhood is lived intrinsically. Old age is felt more discerningly and often negatively. It's a place many of us don't get to visit, yet paradoxically a place easily taken for granted. Old age is often an assumption. We all think we'll get there. Lots of us don't. The part of being old that Grandma likes — being old.

"In the present, we often lose historical perspective," she's saying. "We tend to look back at generations and think of how much we've progressed. We laugh at pictures of people smoking in planes. But what are we doing now that the next generation will find ridiculous ... or destructive? By then it will seem so obvious. Am I making any sense?"

"Yeah," I say. "I understand, you're right."

"I guess what I mean is the future becomes the past pretty quickly."

"So then the only constant is the present."

"And when I think about it, I really can't believe that I'm still around. It doesn't make much sense to me," she says. "George never would have believed it. We always thought I'd be the first to go."

"You're healthy and active and you do things. You still think about things, Grandma."

"It's hard to explain, though. So many in my family died young. Even my dad, who was a healthy guy, he died when I was away at war in Europe. I just never would have imagined living this long, into my nineties."

I've been wanting to ask her more about death. The topic has come up only once, back in my kitchen. It's not an easy thing to casually toss out to someone in their nineties, someone who is so close. What does it feel like to know you've already lived the vast majority of your life, to be one of the last few of your generation? It must feel strange to know death is so near. If I don't ask now, I won't.

"So you don't worry about dying, Grandma? Or even what death is?"

"I don't worry about it, no, never. It's the end of something, that's all we know. What if it's also the start of something, something unimaginable for us now? We just don't know. But we can each have our own ideas about it, and that's what I like. I like that our own impressions and suspicions of death can be so utterly personal. Do you ever think about it?"

"I guess, yeah, sometimes."

"Maybe I should think about it more, but I don't know any more about dying because I'm closer to it than someone younger. We all know the same about dying: nothing. And my entire life, I've never thought much about it. That's not to say I don't think about everyone in my life who's gone before me. My mother, father, sisters, brothers, aunts, uncles, friends. And, of course, George. I do feel like I know the process of dealing with death, its pain. And it is a kind of process," she says. "That's why I left the war, on compassionate leave. I was told I had to go home, back to Canada. Someone in my family had died."

"But you weren't told who?"

"No. And to be honest I thought it was my mother. She'd taken ill before I left. I thought about her all the way back home. When I arrived, I found out it was actually my father."

"So many people around you have died."

"I don't think you ever get used to it, though, or really know how to deal with it. Each time it's different, and hard for different reasons. I guess I'm the last one left. And in some ways that makes the idea of death almost comforting to me. It'll be my turn soon enough. It's just not something to fear or worry about. So I never even think about. When it's my turn, it's my turn," she says. "And that's really all I know."

"I guess you're right," I say.

"The older I get, the more of the future I get to see. I'm still the person I was at nine, just older. So being old like me is being in a position of luck. I think sometimes people assume luck and ease are the same. I don't think they are," she says, stirring cream into her freshened coffee. "Being lucky isn't about constant happiness, things being easy, or always getting what you want."

★

OUTSIDE THE CAFÉ, in the rain, we huddle together under my fickle umbrella and wait.

The rain is falling harder. I think it's falling harder. There's been so much rain this week it's hard to remember when it's been heavy and when it's been light; rain of varying strength has essentially been a constant companion. We're hopeful it might let up.

I'm still considering Grandma's words from lunch, and not just the sentiment. It was her face, her eyes, as she spoke. I watch a guy walking for the bus. He doesn't think he's going to make it, so doesn't bother to speed up. The bus has already disgorged passengers and filled up with new ones; it's lingering. The light hasn't changed. I watch as hope enters the man's body. His next step is swifter. Then, yes, he can make it! He believes! He's going to make it! He starts into a full trot. Four or five strides into his run, the light changes, and the bus spits some cloudy exhaust and abruptly pulls out into traffic. He's about six steps from it. His bag drops off his shoulder. He eases back into a casual walk.

This is life, I think.

"Did you see that?" I ask Grandma. "That guy?"

"Which one, dear?" she asks, looking up at me.

"The one over there, who ran for the bus. He wasn't going to run and then he did. He made the decision to run, but he still didn't make it."

"No, I didn't. Did he miss it?"

"Yup. It was heartbreaking."

"There'll be another, then," she says, hooking her arm into mine. "Shall we brave the rain?"

★

IT'S NOT A café, but coffee is the first thing you smell. There are other smells, too — all pleasant, but none as potent. The fine food store on Brock Street has a creaky wooden floor and an olfactory appeal unmatched in this town. Grandma has been asking about stopping by since her first day in Kingston. We almost forgot. I almost forgot. Grandma remembered during lunch. She wants to take some cheese back with her. Just some aged cheddar cheese is what she said. It seems like a relatively insignificant item to make a special stop for, but I know she loves her cheese.

I'm carrying the handbasket. She's already half-filled it. Inside are a pack of white tea, two chocolate bars, some coffee-flavoured hard candies, organic wheat crackers, and a jar of marmalade. We've yet to make it to the cheese counter.

"Do we need any other snacks for the car?" Grandma asks. "I still have to get my cheese."

"We could probably use something else."

"Well, you go pick something, then."

I leave Grandma at the cheese counter to sniff out the fine selection of fudge, another soft spot for her. I'm no fudge devotee. I have many vice teeth — fatty, salty, caffeiney, alcoholy, etc. — but surprisingly not much of a sweet tooth. And fudge is as sickly sweet as they come. I find it intentionally cloying, borderline offensive in its obviousness as a sweet snack. Yet in the car, especially on road trips, I do covet the odd lump. Its high sucrose content and robust flavour switch from annoying to comforting. This time I go with maple and peanut butter. I furtively pay for them and find Grandma still kicking tires at the cheese display. There are many varieties to choose from.

"Oh, I'm sorry, they all look so good," she says apologetically. "I'm only getting one more." She already has two types of cheese wrapped up beside her. The man wielding the knife is cutting a piece the size of my fist from a cinder block of aged cheddar.

I unload the contents of our basket at the cash. Holding her mob of cheese in both hands, Grandma demands to pay and pushes me aside, debit card in her mouth.

WE (I) NIBBLE on our fudge until it's finished. We've been on the road for an hour or so when Grandma turns and asks if I want to stop for a scratch pad.

"A what?"

"I thought maybe you'd be ready for a scratch pad."

I am trying to understand. Honestly. But I have to ask. "Sorry, what exactly is a scratch pad, Grandma?"

"Oh, isn't that what you call coffees on the road?"

"Right, road coffees. No, I call them goofballs."

She's laughing now. "I never get these things right."

"I think I like scratch pads better."

We pull off the highway and enter the same coffee shop we stopped at on the way down. I park and leave Grandma in the car. It's hard to tell, with the uniforms and visored caps that make everyone look analogous regardless of place, day, or time, but I think it might be the same overly cheery human at the cash who hands me our scratch pads.

Back in the car, I park crookedly in a different spot, this one facing the road. I lower my window a crack, then turn the ignition off. We both release our belts in unison. The paper cup is hot in my hand.

"We'll just wait here for a bit, until the coffee cools."

I remove the plastic lid and drop it on the floor by my feet. Grandma leaves her cup in the holder. Cars and trucks glide by in front of us.

"I never did develop a taste for cards, you know. Especially bridge."

I'm caught slightly off guard by Grandma's arbitrary comment, but now I'm also used to her way of starting a discussion, how something enters her consciousness and she just starts into it.

"Oh, really? I thought you loved playing cards."

"I've played reluctantly, off and on, for most of my life. It's just that I've never loved it. It was just something we did. I usually agreed to games out of a sense of social duty more than anything, if that makes sense. I don't really enjoy playing, but I do have a fondness for bridge. I'd been sharing some tea with my mother and sister when I was called to the phone. This was just after the war. I picked up the receiver and said hello.

"A man introduced himself. His name was George. He told me he got my number from another nurse he'd met on a train. Both were just back from the war. He hoped I didn't mind him calling out of the blue. I told him of course not. This wasn't unusual for the time.

"At the time of the call I didn't know, but George had cut short his engineering studies when war was declared and spent the succeeding years as a navigator on a minesweeper.

But now the war was over. He'd survived. He was travelling by train back to Winnipeg to get his discharge. That was all he knew of his future.

"On the train George was seated next to a woman, an army nurse. They were both in uniform and in good spirits. At some point the nurse told him about her friend who was also a nurse and just happened to be back in Winnipeg. She told him to call me when he got to Winnipeg. It didn't take long for him to move past pleasantries and get to the gist of his call. He wanted to meet. His sister and brother-in-law needed a fourth for bridge. They would be playing later that evening. He asked if I wanted to join.

"I apologized and asked him to wait for a moment before I answered. I'd never played bridge before, Iain. I returned to the kitchen and told my sister and mother. I thought I should probably decline. I didn't even know how to play bridge. All my mother said was, 'Then it's about time you learned.' I went back to the phone and accepted the offer. George said he would be by to pick me up shortly."

"I don't think I knew this. For some reason I thought you'd met Grandpa overseas."

"Well, this wasn't long after getting back. After returning from Europe, I'd gone to work at the Fort Osborne Barracks hospital. Two days after our game of bridge, I finished a long shift and then walked home with a colleague. We decided to stop at a small restaurant for supper. And there was George. He walked right by the table. I called to him, and he came over and said hello."

"Did you know you liked him at this point?"

"I certainly found him handsome. He had short, dark

hair and such a nice face. He was of average height but had sort of a wiry, slender build. He was very strong for his size.

"He asked us both if we'd like to go to the naval mess for a drink. He'd just left a banquet in the hall above the restaurant. It was still going on, but he was feeling restless, bored. He'd been on his way to the phone to ring a friend but said if we were free, he'd prefer our company. We said we'd be happy to join him.

"The mess was busy and loud. That was normal, of course. We each had a drink, then another, and another. I'm not sure, we may have even had another. I was looking at George. I couldn't believe he was six years older than me. If anything, he looked six years younger. I liked the way he talked, the way he laughed."

"You can remember all that?"

"Oh, sure. It was late when we decided to call it a night. I had work the next day and hadn't planned on being out so late. George suggested a taxi. Once we were inside, I was wondering who was going to get dropped off first. My friend lived in a different direction."

"Right," I say, clueing in.

"George was sitting up front, next to the driver, and had told him where to go first. I was pretty happy when we pulled up to my friend's apartment first. We would have some privacy. And the next day, and every day after, I found him waiting for me outside the hospital when my workday was done."

"Every day?"

"Yup, every day. He proposed three weeks and two days after that first night of bridge. I was completely surprised. I paused before answering."

"How come?" I ask.

"I was happy with life. I was happy with my work. I'd put in a request to volunteer, this time in Japan, where the war was still going on. Nurses were needed. It would have been another adventure. But I've never been the type to do something just because it's been planned. Meeting George certainly wasn't planned. It wasn't what I'd been sitting around waiting for, or thinking about."

"What did you say?"

"I said yes, of course."

She'd known him for only three weeks.

"When George told his sister the news, she was aghast. His sister couldn't believe what she was hearing. She didn't know why he was marrying someone he'd known for only a couple of weeks. His sister thought it was ridiculous. He didn't know anything about me."

"Grandpa told you this?"

"Yup, and he had an easy reply for her. He told his sister he was marrying the nurse he didn't know because he loved her. His sister laughed, said it sounded so naive. I guess it probably did. She really thought he was being silly. She didn't think it was like George to be so irrational."

The night they were married, Grandma and Grandpa had known each other for less than five weeks.

"You see, I was just plain lucky to have said yes to that game of bridge. I just knew it, right from when we were married. There was so much we were going to do together. It really was so exciting, Iain, to be at the beginning of something, to be starting out. At one point during our wedding night, George got up to go to the bathroom. He was humming. For some reason I can remember thinking how soft the bed was. He was very musical. I can't believe I remember that."

I've never heard this story before, of how Grandma and Grandpa met.

"Heavens, I should stop going on. And I have something to give you before I forget." She's switched the topic of discussion so quickly I can't react or even comment.

Grandma bends down to the bag on the floor in front of her. She's moving her hand around in the bag like she's randomly drawing a name from a hat. When her hand finds whatever it's fishing for, she brings the bag, with her hand still inside, up to her lap. "Here," she says.

I accept a tiny bottle of gourmet champagne mustard. I recognize it immediately from the fine foods store.

"Didn't you say you love mustard?" she asks, hopefully. "You put some in the meatloaf, right?"

"Yeah, definitely. I love it. And champagne. Thank you. You really didn't have to get me anything. But I also have something for you."

"What? Really?"

"It's nothing. Just, well, a little thank-you."

I reach behind my seat and grab my own bag. I hand her an equally small glass jar of red pepper jelly.

"I always remember having red pepper jelly at your house when we were kids. That was the first place I had it."

"Yes, of course, I love it. Thank you."

For a while we sit with steaming scratch pads in hand and our lampoonishly tiny glass jars of spread in our laps.

"I think I've realized something on our trip," she says.

"I hope you don't mind me saying, but I think you and I are a lot alike. I always thought that, but I'm certain of it now, after these days together."

I look out the windshield. We're sitting in the rain, an hour or so outside my sleepy town, still an hour or so from Grandma's house, in my twenty-year-old car, where it's just been theorized that I might be more similar to a white-haired ninety-two-year-old woman with a bad knee than to anyone else. Beyond being prone to a runny nose when the temperature dips below eight degrees, I'm not convinced there's any truth at all in the claim. It seems too unjust to Grandma. But if there is, even a trace, I will definitely take it.

"We've done pretty well," says Grandma, bringing her paper cup toward me. "To the road trip, my last one."

"The trip," I say, finding my voice, touching her cup with my own.

WE'VE PASSED MANY woodpiles and log barns. Several streams and ponds. Even sparsely inhabited towns with the odd inhabitant walking a dog on the gravel shoulder of the road. The engine is loud. We're quiet.

I've refocused on the road but am glancing over periodically. Grandma's eyelids have dipped shut. I adjust the mix-tape I've put in the deck, turning it down.

"It's okay," she says, keeping her eyes closed. "You can leave it, dear. I like this song. I think that's a piccolo."

She's right; "Rockin' Robin" is a pretty great song. I return the volume to its original setting. I was anticipating a busy ride, with lots of cars and trucks. We've only seen a few. It's because of the rain, I think — that's probably why the road's been empty. People don't like driving in the rain. People would rather stay home.

She's enjoyed our trip, but I'm sensing Grandma is ready to be home. She'll want to unpack and do some laundry. She'll want to get into her garden and go grocery shopping so she can fill her fridge with her favourite foods, some salty, some sweet. She'll be pleased to run into her neighbours, and to feed her old cat treats and rub her ears. She'll have phone messages to return and mail to open. She'll make herself some tea. She'll take a nap on her couch.

"This is probably a stupid question," I say, still looking straight ahead, "but do you have a first conscious memory, Grandma? I've been trying to think of mine as I drive. I can't. I have some memories from when I was around four or five. But they kind of meld together. There's nothing really distinct."

"Yes," she says, "I do."

"Really? What is it?"

"I was four."

"You were in Winnipeg by then?"

"Yes, but we hadn't been there for long. We had a garden in our backyard. There were flowers, but it was mostly for veggies. I remember being outside one morning in the spring. I was alone in the yard. It had been raining. The ground was all wet. I was wearing rubber boots that had probably been my older sister's, because they were too big for me.

"For whatever reason I decided I wanted to explore the garden. I just walked right in to see if anything had started growing yet. The earth was so wet from all the rain that after a few steps I got stuck. The more I wiggled my feet to get loose, the deeper they sunk in. The mud was tight up around my ankles."

"What did you do?" I ask.

"I just stopped moving. Out in the middle of the garden wasn't a bad place to be stuck. I didn't call out to anyone. I just looked around. It wasn't long before my brother Pat must have noticed. I felt two hands come down and lift me up out of the boots. The boots stayed in the mud and he carried me back to the house in my socks. I still remember that."

I glance at Grandma momentarily, then back to the road.

"Well," she says, "it's not much of a story, but it's the first thing I can remember."

She's cracked her window. I'm thinking it's a bit brisk for that while driving. My hands are cold on the wheel. I consider suggesting a roll-up. But when I look over again a few minutes later, she seems to be thoroughly enjoying it, and I resist.

Her breathing has changed; it has slowed. Her head is resting back and to the right. Her eyes might be closed again. The gap is small enough that no rain is getting in, but large enough for the wind to rush in and swirl her thin white hair into disarray. Strands are flailing in different directions, like each is an unmanned fireman's hose.

4:02 p.m.

SO MANY OF the houses on her street, in her neighbourhood, have been renovated in the past few years. The area
has become trendier, but the houses are too small and out-
dated for contemporary taste. People are buying for the
location, gutting pre-existing homes and building their
own, much larger structures. Driveways and garages are
expanding; lawns are shrinking.

Grandma's house is one of the few that remain intact. It
was built just after the war. There's no bulky addition on the
back. She doesn't even have a garage. If I lived here, all the
(unnecessary) change in the neighbourhood would upset
me. I would resent the shift in aesthetics and mentality. I
would be discouraged. But Grandma is not me.

She doesn't endorse these developments but, looking at
her, I can tell she's pleased to be back on her street. It's still
her street. She's sitting up straighter, gazing out her window, down the street toward her house, the one she's lived
in for more than sixty years.

By today's standard it's a small, plain house. The
kitchen and bathroom have never been remodelled. The
dishes, the metal cutlery, pots, and pans are the same; so
are the ornaments, books, framed photos and art, her coffee table, dining table, chairs, and cupboards. Her carpets
are older than I am. For as long as I've known her she's
had a glass jar of caramels and candies on the counter. The
piano in the living room (which Grandpa played) remains
in the same spot it's always been, just to the left of the front
window.

"It looks like we've had lots of rain here, too," she says, running her hand along the floor to retrieve her purse, setting it in her lap. "It will be a good summer for the garden, I bet."

Of everything she's experienced, her own accomplishments, the eras she's lived through, it's still her interest in others that fuels her. Her deep connection to family, friends, and acquaintances has dulled the attenuating effects of time and growing old. When they first moved to the house, in the early fifties, Grandma was in her thirties and the road was unpaved gravel. The ditches were freshly dug. She's lived more than ten years without Grandpa and almost as many without Donald. Both died in their early eighties. She never imagined living this long without them.

She still thinks about Grandpa and Donald, but also, more distinctively, about people she continues to meet, or those she hears or reads about. It's an energy typically reserved for youth. After all her shared years with Grandpa and her own exploits, she doesn't dwell solely in memories. She remains impressed and irritated and upset and touched and interested by people in the present; they nourish her. It's not just about maintaining equilibrium in a circle of close friends. It's relationships, old and new, that enliven her, that remain her connection to the past but also her filter for the future. Her desire for new interactions isn't rooted in politics or ideology or beliefs. It's something I'm aware of only after seeing it for five days. Grandma continues to make brief, unselfish connections with individuals, every day, wherever she goes. What I initially perceived as negligible or incidental encounters I now understand to be intentionally sought and significant.

"By mid-June all these trees on each side of the road will almost touch overhead; some of them will touch. It's almost like we get a temporary leaf canopy every year," she says, "but only for the summer. It's hard to remember when they weren't this tall."

Grandma didn't go to university. She didn't spend four years studying in libraries and great halls. She's never sat in on a calculus class, literary theory course, or philosophy tutorial. She's never waited after a lecture to talk with a professor about the specifics of a lesson.

I'm not sure I completely understand or even feel comfortable attempting to unravel it. I've been thinking about it on our drive: Grandma is profoundly smart.

She is smart beyond the cliché of emotional intelligence. Intelligence is so often perceived and explained in blunt, rudimentary ways. We decide someone is astute based on a certain career choice or educational path. We call some people bright and others dim. We say someone is logical or mathematically minded, while someone else is creative or imaginative. We deem some "book smart," others "street smart." Sometimes we speak of positive attitudes and admire those who are able to look on the bright side.

Grandma's disposition can only be fully appreciated after moving beyond those basic platitudes. Hers is a rare intelligence, more complex than a positive outlook, obsession with reason, or comprehension of complex principles. It is neither masculine nor feminine. It's not forceful, pretentious, or judgemental. It's subtle and modest. It's outward, not inward. Grandma's is a practical aptitude, a salient social dexterity. It is a compassionate toughness. She knows and accepts both happiness and sadness, how each is reliant on the other.

She's comfortable with all that is unintelligible. Her mental currency is reality, not abstraction or invention or apprehension. She just knows how to exist in her world. At ninety-two, Grandma is very old and she is very alive. She lives.

I can see the single maple tree on her lawn as her red-brick house comes into view.

"Well, well," she says. "After all that, and here we are."

Here we are.

ACKNOWLEDGEMENTS

Thank you:

Samantha Haywood and Janie Yoon, for all the indispensable contributions.

Everyone at House of Anansi, my sister for her editorial eye, Mark Medley, Peter Norman, Kenneth Anderton, and the Ontario Arts Council.

My family, for continued encouragement and support.

Grandma. For our chats and everything else.

IAIN REID is the author of the critically acclaimed and award-winning comic memoir *One Bird's Choice*, which was published in several languages and sold internationally. He was named by the *Globe and Mail* as a top five up-and-coming Canadian author. He writes regularly about books and writing for the *National Post*. He lives in Kingston, Ontario.